BACK 2 GOD

America's Last Chance

Dexter D. Sanders

authorHOUSE®

AuthorHouse™
1663 Liberty Drive
Bloomington, IN 47403
www.authorhouse.com
Phone: 1 (800) 839-8640

Published by AuthorHouse 10/30/2015

ISBN: 978-1-5049-5747-2 (sc)
ISBN: 978-1-5049-5746-5 (e)

Library of Congress Control Number: 2015917434

Print information available on the last page.

This book is printed on acid-free paper.

Dedication

This book is dedicated to you IF:
You are a child of the Most High God

This book is dedicated to you IF:
You represent the remnant of God's people that are not afraid to stand up for Him

This book is dedicated to you IF:
You are the redeemed of the Lord ready to "Say NO"

This book is dedicated to you IF:
You are ready and willing to stand up and say "No" to abortions

This book is dedicated to you IF:
You are ready and willing to stand up and say "NO" to same sex marriage

This book is dedicated to you IF:
You are ready and willing to say "NO" to the notion that homosexuality is normal, natural and healthy

This book is dedicated to you IF:
You are ready and willing to stand up and say "NO" to Government intrusion and control

This book is dedicated to you IF:
You are willing to humble, pray, seek and turn "Back 2 God"

2 Chronicles 2:7-14 (NKJV)
14 if My people who are called by My name will humble themselves, and pray and seek My face, and turn from their wicked ways, then I will hear from heaven, and will forgive their sin and heal their land.

Contents

A Personal Note From the Author

The strangest thing happened to me one day. It was Saturday evening and a good friend of mine by the name of Ted Knaak invited me to go to a meeting. I had no idea what type of meeting we were going to, but I trusted Ted's judgment. As we were getting closer to our destination, Ted shared with me that we were going to a Tea Party meeting. I looked at Ted and asked if he were crazy. Are you kidding me? Dexter DeWayne Sanders, at a Tea Party meeting? You see, up to that point everything I'd ever heard about the Tea Party was very negative, especially as it pertained to African-American people. By then we were at the facility and the meeting started, so I decided to trust my friend and go inside.

Once inside I began listening to the first speaker, he talked about the need to up our fight against abortion clinics popping up all over Central Florida. I found myself applauding that speaker. The next speaker talked about our need to fight against government intrusion. He talked about the negative impact welfare and entitlement programs were having on people across the nation. I found myself applauding that speaker as well. The third and last speaker suggested that we take a stand against the same-sex marriage political agenda, aimed at discrediting the Bible and rewriting the definition of marriage. By now I was standing on my feet applauding.

Then the unthinkable happened, the facilitator of the meeting announced: Pastor Dexter Sanders is in the audience, and he asked if I would say a few words. I can't tell you how I felt at that moment. There were 150 to 200 people in that room and they were all white except for myself and one other black woman. I had no idea what to say, but God showed up and spoke through me. I found myself talking from the abundance of experience I had ministering to the homeless on the streets of Orlando, Florida. Having set up free transitional housing for both men and women, who said they were serious about turning their lives around, I discovered we had good hearts and intentions, but the wrong strategy. During those years I discovered handouts didn't work. In fact they may have done more harm than good.

While I was standing there talking, I suggested that maybe our president had the same problem; a good heart but the wrong strategy. Now I'm convinced that he has neither good heart nor strategy. Before I knew it, the 200 people in that room were standing on their feet. However, they were unaware of the work God was doing to change my heart at that very moment.

As you read this book you'll discover that I'm very passionate about the idea that we need to get "Back 2 God". At one point in my life I was the pastor preaching the gospel, evangelizing, sharing the Word of God. At the same time, I was the guy in November who would go into the voting booth and vote for candidates that did not represent my faith. As a matter of fact, I voted for a president that supports the notion that homosexuality is normal, natural and healthy. I voted for a president that helped usher same-sex marriage into America. I voted for a president who believes killing innocent babies is all right.

God convicted me that day and I promised Him that I would never vote for another person simply because they had the same color skin as me. I also promised to never again support anyone who was not willing to stand up for the principles, morals and values found in the Bible. During that time, God brought an interesting question to my mind; if you Dexter Sanders, who is not the smartest guy in the world, but with a Bachelor's and two Masters Degrees, you certainly are not the dumbest. If you could walk around in such deep ignorance, imagine the millions of God fearing people across this nation, black, white or Hispanic, who are not bad people, but simply misinformed and ignorant to their responsibility to God, to stand up for His principles.

That's when God gave me a new assignment and the "Back 2 God" movement was born. Today and every day, my life is dedicated to sharing the "Back 2 God" message, to empower and encourage God's people, the redeemed of the Lord to stand up for God in this nation!

Introduction

Anyone who knows anything about me knows that what I love to do most is share the life-changing gospel of Jesus Christ to our brothers and sisters who are the least, the last, and the lost. However, in these United States of America, most people have already heard the life-changing gospel of Jesus Christ. Most people have already been exposed to His teachings. Having been exposed, most people have already chosen to either accept or reject God's word. So today I'm not here to share the love, mercy, and grace that is inherent in the word of God. Instead, I'm here to remind those people who have accepted Jesus Christ as their Lord and Savior of who and whose they are.

You might be asking, "Why does Dexter Sanders believe we, the children of the Most High God, the Christian nation in the United States of America, need reminding of anything?" I'm here to remind you because clearly many of us have forgotten. Look at the condition of this great country, the land of the free and the home of the brave. Lately it looks more like the land of the hopeless and the home of the forgotten. We're hopeless due to our insistence to not include God in our daily living. In fact, He has now begun to turn His back on us the way we've turned our backs on Him.

This book, *Back 2 God*, suggests two things, the first being that we as individuals need to get back to God. What does that mean?

Genesis 1:26–27 says, **"Then God said, 'Let Us make man in Our image, according to Our likeness; let them have dominion over the fish of the sea, over the birds of the air, and over the cattle, over all**

the earth and over every creeping thing that creeps on the earth.' So God created man in His *own* image; in the image of God He created him; male and female He created them" (emphasis added). What many people do not understand is that from the moment God said, essentially, "**Let us create man,"** all of humankind was created. Most of us would like to think that our birthdays signify the days we were born to our mothers and fathers. However, that's only partly true. Yes, we celebrate birthdays according to when we went to the hospital and actually came through our mothers' canals into the world. That birthday, however, is a physical birthday. Our spiritual birthdays happened the day God said, "Let us make man."

The timing of when we were conceived in our mothers' wombs was God's; He decides when our spiritual bodies should take on flesh. Our mothers and fathers, after engaging in intercourse, created our physical bodies. Our spiritual bodies, which were created at the beginning of time, simply joined our physical bodies at conception. What's important for us to understand is that while we were spirits without flesh, we were in perfect harmony with God. We were without sin and were one with God the Father, God the Son, and God the Holy Spirit. When we took on flesh, we took on sin, which separated us from God.

Our very souls long to be back in perfect relationship with God. This explains the war in our minds between good and evil. Our souls want to reunite with God and experience the oneness we had in the beginning. However, the flesh, being of this world and evil, fights against the soul. God, because He loves us so much, put together a plan whereby we could reunite with Him and get "back to God." In order to execute His plan, God sent His only Son, Jesus Christ, to die for our sins. Our only responsibility is to believe that He (Jesus) is the Son of the living God and that He died for us that we might be reunited with God.

The second thing this book suggests is that it is time for this whole country to get back to God. What do I mean by that? This country was founded on godly principles, but lately it has experienced spiritual moral decline, turned its back on God, and moved away from His principles,

His values, and His perfect will. Consequently, we've watched our country deteriorate as our communities have been infested with drugs, alcohol, prostitution, homosexuality, and the like. We've watched our schools move from institutions that honor God and educational endeavors to places that have to be more concerned about keeping children alive. We've watched our government go from one that was founded and centered on godly principles to one that attempts to remove God from every aspect of our lives.

In short, the United States of America is in big trouble. I tell this joke wherever I speak: "Even Ray Charles and Stevie Wonder can see that our country is in big trouble!" The interesting thing is that we didn't start off this way. Yes, we have had some ugly bumps along the road, such as our nation's struggle with the issue of slavery. But by the 1800s there were clear signs that we were dedicated to being a godly nation. Our forefathers founded this country with God as the center. Since 1864 all our currency has read "In God We Trust." This notion comes straight from the word of God.

You know what Proverbs 3:5–6 says: **"Trust in the Lord with all your heart, And lean not on your own understanding; In all your ways acknowledge Him, And He shall direct your paths."** We were going to be a nation that trusted the Lord rather than ourselves, a nation that would not lean on our understanding but on God's understanding, purpose, morals, values, and plan. You see, we were on the right track.

In 1954 the Pledge of Allegiance incorporated the words "one nation under God," meaning we would be a nation that honored God. God would be the center of everything that we accomplished in this country. In 1956 "In God We Trust" was established as our national motto. We started out the right way, but things began to go south rather quickly.

The remainder of this book will show how God blessed this country to become the greatest nation in history and how we turned our backs on God. God will also help us understand what we need to do to get back to Him.

Back 2 God accompanies the "Back 2 God Movement. The movement strives to make people aware that now is the last chance for the United States of America to turn its will back to God. The movement is an outward expression of God's love for us. He does not want this country to be destroyed. He does not want what was the apple of His eye to experience this downward spiral into a cesspool of sin. He wants to save this country, and He wants to save each of us. So this book and this movement is for the redeemed of the Lord, those of us who have said yes to Jesus Christ but are not yet walking in the power and authority that He has given us.

1

Put *Us* Back in *USA*

It's time to put *us* back in *USA*. However, first we must first put God back into the USA. God was once the center of the United States of America, but at some point He was taken out. Or to put it a different way, the United States of America turned its back on God.

My task is to prove that indeed God was the center of this nation's development. God was the reason the Pilgrims left England to come to this country. In order to better understand why the Pilgrims would leave England in the first place, it is necessary to understand England's religious climate at the time.

The year was 1534, and England had just broken ties with the Catholic Church. This was an opportunity for people of the Protestant faith who thought reform was necessary to bounce into action and bring true reform. Because of their desire to bring "purity" to the church, these people became known as Puritans. The Puritans wanted to get away from the practices of the Catholic Church that they knew were not biblical. After trying for many years without success, some of the Puritans decided that enough was enough. It was time to separate from the Church of England.

As a result, a new group emerged that would become known as the Separatists. The Puritans and the Separatists shared the same theological views and beliefs. The difference was that some of the Puritans decided to stay in the Church of England, while the Separatists decided to separate.

The Separatists later became known as the Pilgrims and would make colonial America their new home.

I should mention that this was not an easy transition for the Separatists, simply because the church and the state in England were one entity. Anyone going against these traditions was considered to be a lawbreaker, punishable by imprisonment and/or persecution. This turned out to be the major reason why in 1609 a small group of Separatists would decide to leave England and sail—not to America but to Holland.

When they arrived in Holland, the Pilgrims enjoyed religious freedom, as they were able to worship and praise our Lord and Savior Jesus Christ without persecution. However, the downside of their move to Holland was that they lived in poverty. There were not many jobs in Holland, and the jobs available offered low pay. As a result, the Pilgrims began to age much quicker and suffered physical setbacks.

If that were not enough, they also began to see their children move away from the teachings of the Bible toward those of other children in Holland. William Bradford, a passenger on the *Mayflower* and later governor of the Plymouth Colony, saw firsthand the negative impact the Dutch culture was having on the Pilgrims as they lived in Holland. He explains it this way:

> Of all the sorrows most heavy to be borne [in Holland] was that many of the children, influenced by these conditions, and the great licentiousness of the young people of the country, and the many temptations of the city, were led by evil example into dangerous courses, getting the reins off their necks and leaving their parents. Some became soldiers, others embarked upon voyages by sea and others upon worse courses tending to dissoluteness and the danger of their souls, to the great grief of the parents and

> the dishonour of God. So they saw their posterity would be in danger to degenerate and become corrupt.[1]

Another important issue for the Pilgrims was their desire to share the life-changing gospel of Jesus Christ to people who made up the least, the last, and the lost. They began to believe that in order to share the message of hope through Christ Jesus, they would need to go to another place, a place that would give them an opportunity to prosper and build the kingdom of God. William Bradford put it this way: "They cherished a great hope and inward zeal of laying good foundations, or at least of making some way towards it, for the propagation and advance of the gospel of the kingdom of Christ in the remote parts of the world, even though they should be but stepping stones to others in the performance of so great a work."[2]

So for these reasons the Pilgrims set out for America. They were well aware of the great sacrifice the task required. That sacrifice was realized when, by the end of the first winter in America, about half the people who came over on the *Mayflower* were dead. Yet this would not deter the remaining Pilgrims who pledged their lives for a chance at religious freedom and prosperity. These few Pilgrims would become the foundation upon which the United States of America would be born. Because of the Pilgrims' commitment and resolve, God Almighty poured out blessings on them, which would result in their building the greatest country ever known to humankind.

Without question, the Pilgrims came to the land that would become our nation for two reasons. The first was to freely worship and serve our Lord and Savior Jesus Christ. The second was to have an opportunity to experience prosperity in this new land. Both became a reality, as the United States of America, once established, became the richest and most powerful nation in history. Clearly God was the motivation for creating and building the United States of America.

---

[1] William Bradford,_*Bradford's History of the Plymouth Settlement,_1608–1650.* Rendered into Modern English by Harold Paget (Boston: E. P. Dutton & Company, 1920), 21.

[2] *Bradford's History*, 21.

There is other evidence that makes us understand that this nation was one founded with God Almighty in mind. Some of the most compelling evidence comes from the founding fathers of our nation. History teaches us that they had deep religious convictions that were based largely in their belief and understanding of the Christian faith in Christ Jesus. There were fifty-six men who signed the Declaration of Independence, and of those men twenty-four held degrees from either Bible schools or seminaries. We need only search the writings of our founding fathers to find evidence that the Christian faith largely influenced the writings of both the Declaration of Independence and the United States Constitution.

George Washington
First US President
"While we are zealously performing the duties of good citizens and soldiers, we certainly ought not to be inattentive to the higher duties of religion. To the distinguished character of Patriot, it should be our highest glory to add the more distinguished character of Christian."[3]

John Adams
Second US President and Signer of the Declaration of Independence
"Suppose a nation in some distant Region should take the Bible for their only law Book, and every member should regulate his conduct by the precepts there exhibited! Every member would be obliged in conscience, to temperance, frugality, and industry; to justice, kindness, and charity towards his fellow men; and to piety, love, and reverence toward Almighty God … What a Eutopia, what a Paradise would this region be."[4]

"The general principles, on which the Fathers achieved independence, were the only Principles in which that beautiful Assembly of young Gentlemen could Unite, and these Principles only could be intended by them in their address, or by me in my answer. And what were these general Principles? I answer, the general Principles of Christianity, in which all these Sects were United: And the general Principles of English and American Liberty, in

---

[3] *The Writings of Washington*, 342–343.
[4] *Diary and Autobiography of John Adams*, Vol. 3, 9.

which all those young Men United, and which had United all Parties in America, in Majorities sufficient to assert and maintain her Independence.

"Now I will avow, that I then believe, and now believe, that those general Principles of Christianity, are as eternal and immutable, as the Existence and Attributes of God; and that those Principles of Liberty, are as unalterable as human Nature and our terrestrial, mundane System."[5]

"The second day of July, 1776, will be the most memorable epoch in the history of America. I am apt to believe that it will be celebrated by succeeding generations as the great anniversary Festival. It ought to be commemorated, as the Day of Deliverance, by solemn acts of devotion to God Almighty. It ought to be solemnized with pomp and parade, with shows, games, sports, guns, bells, bonfires and illuminations, from one end of this continent to the other, from this time forward forever."[6]

Thomas Jefferson
Third US President, Drafter and Signer of the Declaration of Independence

"God who gave us life gave us liberty. And can the liberties of a nation be thought secure when we have removed their only firm basis, a conviction in the minds of the people that these liberties are of the Gift of God? That they are not to be violated but with His wrath? Indeed, I tremble for my country when I reflect that God is just; that His justice cannot sleep forever; That a revolution of the wheel of fortune, a change of situation, is among possible events; that it may become probable by Supernatural influence! The Almighty has no attribute which can take side with us in that event."[7]

"I am a real Christian—that is to say, a disciple of the doctrines of Jesus Christ."[8]

---

[5] Letter to Thomas Jefferson, June 28, 1813.

[6] Letter to Abigail Adams, July 3, 1776.

[7] *Notes on the State of Virginia, Query XVIII*, 237.

[8] *The Writings of Thomas Jefferson*, 385.

John Hancock
First Signer of the Declaration of Independence
"Resistance to tyranny becomes the Christian and social duty of each individual. ... Continue steadfast and, with a proper sense of your dependence on God, nobly defend those rights which heaven gave, and no man ought to take from us."[9]

Benjamin Franklin
Signer of the Declaration of Independence and Unites States Constitution
"Here is my Creed. I believe in one God, the Creator of the Universe. That He governs it by His Providence. That He ought to be worshipped.

"That the most acceptable service we render to him is in doing good to his other children. That the soul of man is immortal, and will be treated with justice in another life respecting its conduct in this. These I take to be the fundamental points in all sound religion, and I regard them as you do in whatever sect I meet with them.

"As to Jesus of Nazareth, my opinion of whom you particularly desire, I think the system of morals and his religion, as he left them to us, is the best the world ever saw, or is likely to see;

"But I apprehend it has received various corrupting changes, and I have, with most of the present dissenters in England, some doubts as to his divinity; though it is a question I do not dogmatize upon, having never studied it, and think it needless to busy myself with it now, when I expect soon an opportunity of knowing the truth with less trouble. I see no harm, however, in its being believed, if that belief has the good consequence, as probably it has, of making his doctrines more respected and more observed; especially as I do not perceive, that the Supreme takes it amiss, by distinguishing the unbelievers in his government of the world with any peculiar marks of his displeasure."[10]

---

[9] *History of the United States of America*, Vol. 2, 229.
[10] Letter to Ezra Stiles, March 9, 1790.

It is clear that the beliefs of the pilgrims who came over, coupled with the spiritual convictions and Christian beliefs of the founding fathers, provide sufficient evidence that the United States of America was born from and formed with Christian biblical beliefs. So where did we go wrong? How did we get from being a nation centered around the things of God to a nation on the fast track to hell? It's time to put *us* back in the *USA*!

2

Where Did We Go Wrong?

As I stated earlier, this nation started off the right way, with God as our center. However, by the early 1900s there was clear evidence that an evil undercurrent existed whose goal was to destroy the United States of America by removing God from our conscience. That's right, there was an evil plan designed and implemented to remove God from this nation. A good friend to conservative America by the name of Cleon Skousen exposed this evil plot in a 1958 in a publication he wrote called *The Naked Communists*. In that publication Skousen exposed the enemy's forty-five-point plan to take God out of United States of America.

The plan was to "breakdown cultural standards of morality by promoting pornography and obscenity and books, magazines, motion pictures, radio and television."[1] Has this already happened in this country? Of course it has; today we are hard pressed to turn on the television or radio without obscenities, vulgar language, and naked bodies confronting us from advertisements and even family television shows. What you need to understand is that this did not show up today or yesterday, and it didn't fall from the sky. It was a part of the enemy's strategic, systematic plan to take God out of this country.

Let's look at the next point from Skousen's publication. He writes that the plan was also to "present homosexuality, degeneracy and promiscuity as

[1] Communist Goals (1963) Congressional Record--Appendix, pp. A34-A35 January 10, 1963

normal, natural and healthy."[2] Has this already happened in the United States of America? You're darn right it has! Just look at the gay-rights political agenda that has become a social and political monster in this country. It is geared to destroy the very family structure that God Almighty created. Our children are being introduced to homosexuality in public schools. Our churches are performing same-sex marriages. What you need to understand is this too did not fall from the sky or come around the corner yesterday. It was part of the enemy's strategic, systematic plan to take God out of this country.

Let's look at another point from the publication. Skousen also writes that the plan was to "infiltrate the churches and replace revealed religion with social religion. Discredit the Bible and emphasize the need for intellectual maturity, that does not need a religious crutch."[3] Is this already happening in the United States of America? You're darn right is! As I just mentioned, the pastors of American churches are performing same-sex marriages.

According to Skousen, the plan was also to: "eliminate prayer or any phase of religious expression in schools, on the ground that it violates the principle of separation of church and state."[4] Has this already happened in the United States of America? You're darn right it has! Madeline O'Hair went on a one-woman campaign to remove prayer from schools. Some say she was a Wiccan, while others say she was an atheist, all I know is she did not love the lord. This one woman went on a campaign and removed prayer from all public schools in this country. You see, that's how I know for a fact that one person can make a difference.

A year later, a man by the name of Eddie Schempp went on a one-man campaign to remove the Bible from all public schools. He wanted to remove the Bible because the Bible teaches moral lessons, such as do to others as you would have done to you, love your neighbor, do not kill, and do not steal. This one man was successful in removing the Bible from our schools.

---

[2] Communist Goals (1963) Congressional Record

[3] Communist Goals (1963)

[4] Communist Goals (1963)

This did not just fall from the sky either, nor did it suddenly appear yesterday. It too was part of the enemy's strategic, systematic plan to take God out of the United States of America Let's take a look at one more of Skousen's insights. He said the plan was to "discredit the American Constitution by calling it inadequate, old-fashioned, out of step with modern needs, offender is of cooperation between nations on a worldwide basis."[5]

Has this already happened in our country? You're darn right has! If you simply open your eyes you will see clearly that our Constitution is under attack. It's under attack by a socialist government dedicated to destroying the fabric of our Constitution and rendering it inadequate for the very purpose of replacing it with laws that go against God.

Those of us who are in Christ Jesus need to be reminded of who we are in Christ because the enemy's plan to remove God from our country worked. How do we know it worked?

Just look at our schools, as they are broken. There are no longer institutions of higher education. Rather, there are places where young people are exposed to common core and introduced to the teachings of Islam more so than Christianity.

Just look at our families, as they are broken. Today more couples who are in Christ Jesus get divorced than those who are not. Just look at our communities, as our communities are broken. They are infested with drugs, alcohol, prostitution, and homosexuality. Just look at our government, as our government is broken. It is being run into the ground by a liberal agenda that wants to lead our nation into socialism.

We have wandered far away from the moral values of God Almighty. Nothing articulates our departure from God better than the word of God itself. If we take a close look at Isaiah 59, we find the great prophet Isaiah describing the condition of God's nation Israel. Upon closer examination, we begin to understand that Isaiah is not just talking about Israel but any

---

[5] Communist Goals (1963)

nation that turns its back on God. In other words, he's describing the United States of America.

Look at Isaiah 59:1, which says, **"Behold, the Lord's hand is not shortened, That it cannot save; Nor His ear heavy, That it cannot hear."** The Bible says God can both hear us and save us. So if God can both hear and save us, why are we in the condition we are in today?

We get the answer to our question in verse 2: **"But your iniquities have separated you from your God; And your sins have hidden *His* face from you, So that He will not hear."** According to this verse our iniquities, or our sins, have separated us from God. God is there, but He's not listening to this country, because this country is no longer listening to Him.

Look at verse 3**: "For your hands are defiled with blood, And your fingers with iniquity; Your lips have spoken lies, Your tongue has muttered perversity."** This is the present state of our country. Our hands are defiled by the blood of African Americans, Native Americans, unborn children, and anyone else who has stood in the way of European settlers and their descendants gaining power. As this country has gained more power, its citizens have begun to think they don't need God. Verse 3 goes on to say, **"Your lips have spoken lies, Your tongue has muttered perversity."** The lies we speak today are against God, as we've moved Him out of our schools and now are trying to move Him out of our government and even our personal lives.

Look at verse 4: **"No one calls for justice, Nor does *any* plead for truth. They trust in empty words and speak lies; They conceive evil and bring forth iniquity."** Isaiah describes a nation no longer concerned with justice, a nation no longer interested in truth—again, he describes a nation like ours. According to the great prophet, we trust in empty words and speak lies. We conceive evil and bring forth sin. This means that we've gone so far away from God that we have become creators of the things that go against God's will.

Look at what God's word says about us as a result of our disobedience and pride. **"Therefore justice is far from us, Nor does righteousness overtake us; We look for light, but there is darkness! For brightness, *but* we walk in blackness!"** (Isaiah 59:9). Justice is far from the United States of America, and there's no righteousness in us at all. Such to the point that even as we look for righteousness, even as we look toward the light, we can still see nothing but darkness. Translated, this suggests that God has given us over to our own sins to the point where even if we tried to do good, it would turn out bad.

Then, as if matters were not bad enough, verses 13–14 give us a clear view of how our trespasses have moved us away from God: **"In transgressing and lying against the Lord, And departing from our God, Speaking oppression and revolt, Conceiving and uttering from the heart words of falsehood. Justice is turned back, And righteousness stands afar off; For truth is fallen in the street, And equity cannot enter."** Because we have transgressed against and lied to our God, we have departed from him. Because we spoke oppression and revolt, we have spoken words of falsehood. Because of our sins against God, justice has been turned back from the United States of America, and all of God's righteousness now stands far away. There is no truth left in our cities, states, or country. We've become a country lost and turned out, content with just doing what we want to do when we want to do it and ignoring God's commands for our lives. To this God is saying, "Just do your thing."

3

It's Up to You and Me

How do I know we need to be reminded of who we are in Christ Jesus? Simple: we are the ones responsible for sitting back and allowing the enemy to wreak havoc on our country, families, and church. God gave us power and dominion over everything. He left us in charge of this great nation.

Because I'm sure that someone reading this book is from the Show Me State, allow me to show you through the word of God. **"Then God said, 'let us make man in our image, according to our likeness; let them have dominion over the fish of the sea, over the birds of the air, and over the, over all the earth and over every creeping thing that creeps on the earth'"** (Genesis 1:26). There are two things that God wants us to see in this scripture. First, we were created in the image of God! I need to let that sink in for a while, because we have a hard time seeing ourselves this way. So let me say it again: we were created in the image of God! Oh my God! God is a God of strength, might, and power. God said to the sun, appear, it appeared. God said to the moon, glow, and it glowed. God told earth and water to separate, and it happened simply because God said it.

God is God Almighty, and you and I were created it His image. We were created to be mighty beings, so there is no way in the world you and I should be pushed around or tossed to and fro by the enemy. As I said, you've got to know who you are and whose you are. We are children of the most high God, and the time has come for us to stand up and act accordingly.

The second thing God wants you to notice in Genesis 1:26 is **"let them have dominion over the fish of the sea, over the birds of the air, and over the cattle, over all the earth and over every creeping thing that creeps on the earth."** Not only were we created in the image of God, but He also gave us dominion over the fish, birds, cattle, and all the earth. *All* means all!

That means we have dominion over our schools. No government can come in and tell us if we can have prayer and the Bible in schools; we're in charge of it.

We have dominion over our communities. No government can come in and tell us what to do with our families or decide what health-care plan we can have or not have. No government can tell us where to live and how to live; we're in charge of it.

We have dominion over our government. Our constitution says, "We the people." That means we the people are in charge of the government. We don't work for the government; the government works for us. We are in charge of it.

Although God left us in charge, we've given our authority over to a corrupt government. We've given our authority over to a corrupt system hell-bent on removing every God concept from this nation and rendering it a godless state.

If God is a mighty God and we were created in His image, then why are we staggering around and watching the enemy kick our butts, take our families, destroy our schools, and hijack our government? It simply does not make sense. The only way it makes sense is if we really do not understand who we are as God's children or the power and authority that He has given to each of us.

God calls for those of us who have said yes to Jesus Christ to stand up for His principles in this country. After all, we are the redeemed of the Lord.

We are the ones who God Almighty pulled out of the cesspool of sin and made His children.

The United States of America needs to stop acting like a little punk! I know; this is the kind of vernacular you might hear on the streets. On the streets, a punk is someone you can walk over, a person who is so afraid, he or she won't take up for himself or herself. This person is not only scared, but he or she also won't stand up for anyone, not even family or friends.

What I'm suggesting is that this great nation—which has the biggest army, the biggest navy, with the Marine Corps, Navy Seals, and more resources than any other country in the world—is acting like a punk. To be a little clearer, I'm suggesting that this nation's Conservative Christian population is acting like a punk.

We have already established that God gave us dominion over this earth, this country, these states, and our cities. For whatever reason, we've stood back on the sidelines and allowed satan, through a Liberal government, to treat us like little chumps. This message is for people both young and old to stand up and stop acting like punks. What is God asking us to stand up to? The answer is simple: we are to stand up to everything that goes against the word of God! If this country means anything to us, it's not time to be afraid or scared. After all, fear is not of the Lord.

Now is the time for us to stand up as the people of God and reclaim our country. The Bible says "there is nothing new under the sun." That being the case, we are not the first people to allow the enemy to push and shove us around. The Bible gives us a story of a punk who just happens to be a king of God's holy people Israel. In this story we will see the heart of a people who will stand up and say, "Stop being a punk." This is a people who stand up for God.

"Now Ben-Hadad the king of Syria gathered all his forces together; thirty-two kings *were* with him, with horses and chariots. And he went up and besieged Samaria, and made war against it. Then he sent messengers into the city to Ahab king of Israel, and said to him, "Thus

says Ben-Hadad: 'Your silver and your gold are mine; your loveliest wives and children are mine'" (1 Kings 20:1–3 NKJV). These verses tell us about the king of Syria, who combines forces with thirty-two other kings and makes war against the country of Samaria. After his victorious battle against Samaria, the king of Syria, Ben-Hadad, sends a message to the king of Israel. He tells the king of Israel, named Ahab, that his silver, his gold, the loveliest of his wives, and his children now belong to him. In other words, Ben-Hadad, the king of Syria, punks Ahab, God's king of Israel.

The story continues in verse 4: **"And the king of Israel answered and said, 'My lord, O king, just as you say, I and all that I have are yours'"** (NKJV) Can you believe this? Look at the way Ahab responds. What a little punk! He doesn't want to fight for what belongs to him—not for his riches or his wives or his children. He just simply says, "Whatever you want to take from me, you can." This is similar to how we behave as the redeemed of the Lord in this country. So far we've been satisfied with allowing satan, through this Liberal government, to take away every God-given right that we have as citizens of this nation.

The people of this country have said no to same-sex marriage, but the government has overruled. The people of this nation are saying no to a common core curriculum in schools, but the government is trying to overrule. Meanwhile, Conservative Christians are sitting back on the sidelines and allowing this to play out. In short, they (we!) are acting like a bunch of punks.

Next let's look at verses 5–6: **"Then the messengers came back and said, 'Thus speaks Ben-Hadad, saying, "Indeed I have sent to you, saying, 'You shall deliver to me your silver and your gold, your wives and your children'; but I will send my servants to you tomorrow about this time, and they shall search your house and the houses of your servants. And it shall be, that whatever is pleasant in your eyes, they will put it in their hands and take it"'"** (NKJV). Ben-Hadad begins insulting Ahab by threatening to take his riches, his wives, and his children. Because the king of Israel sits back and allows the enemy to disrespect him and threaten him, Ben-Hadad now decides to take even more. This is exactly what has happened to the United States of America. Systematically, the enemy has taken from us little by little. Roe v. Wade allowed abortions to be conducted in this country. Madaline O'Hara decided to go on a one-woman campaign to remove prayer from schools, and she was victorious. Because we didn't stand up in the beginning, now this Liberal government wants to take more.

Let's look next at verse 7: **"So the king of Israel called all the elders of the land, and said, 'Notice, please, and see how this man seeks trouble, for he sent to me for my wives, my children, my silver, and my gold; and I did not deny him'"** (NKJV). The one thing the king does right is consult his elders, but he admits that he had been willing to sit back and allow the enemy to take from him the things that God had blessed him with. Such is the case with our country today: we, the Christian nation, find ourselves sitting on the sidelines as the enemy comes to steal, kill, and destroy, and he's succeeding.

Look at verse 8: **"And all the elders and all the people said to him, 'Do not listen or consent'"** (NKJV). This verse tells us that the elders advised the king of Israel to not listen or consent. In other words, the king was advised to stand up and fight rather than allow the enemy to freely take what God had given him and the nation of Israel. Likewise, let this serve as advice to Conservative Christians of the United States of America. Do not sit back and allow the same-sex marriage political agenda to take over our country. Do not sit back and allow this Liberal government to dictate how we live in this country. The time is here and the time is now for us to stand up and fight.

Look at verse 9: "**Therefore he said to the messengers of Ben-Hadad, 'Tell my lord the king, "All that you sent for to your servant the first time I will do, but this thing I cannot do."' And the messengers departed and brought back word to him"** (NKJV). Just when we thought it couldn't get any worse, the king of Israel tells the enemy, "I'll give you your first request, but the second one I can't do." Can you believe this? "You can still have my gold, my silver, and my wife, but you can't have anything else." Remember, this is the king of Israel, the king of God's chosen nation, willing to allow his enemy to take his wives, children, and riches. In many ways America is no different. We too have been willing to sit back and allow our enemy to destroy the lives of our children and families.

Look at verses 10–11: **"Then Ben-Hadad sent to him and said, 'The gods do so to me, and more also, if enough dust is left of Samaria for a handful for each of the people who follow me.' So the king of Israel answered and said, 'Tell him, "Let not the one who puts on his armor boast like the one who takes it off"'"** (NKJV). The two kings exchange insults, which indicates that by this point, at least, the king of Israel is brave enough to speak against his enemy.

Notice in verse 12 that after he speaks, something happens: **"And it happened when Ben-Hadad heard this message, as he and the kings were drinking at the command post, that he said to his servants, 'Get ready.' And they got ready to attack the city"** (NKJV). Notice two things: First, notice the king of Israel's enemies are drinking, which means they were not at all worried about him and his army. For good reason, up until this point, Ahab had not revealed himself to be a threat. Second, notice that the Ben-Hadad makes a decision to attack, which is probably not the best choice seeing that he and his servants have been drinking.

Look at verse 13: **"Suddenly a prophet approached Ahab king of Israel, saying, 'Thus says the Lord: "Have you seen all this great multitude? Behold, I will deliver it into your hand today, and you shall know that I am the Lord"** (NKJV). God sends a messenger, a prophet, to reassure His people of victory if they are willing to stand. Despite the fact that Ben-Hadad has thirty-two kings with him, and despite the fact that he has more men and more power than King Ahab, God says, "I'm going to empower you to win." If God is for you, who can be against you? This is what we need to understand as God's warriors. If we will stand up against the enemy in this country, God will fight this battle for us. God is only waiting for a few good men and women to stand up in faith, knowing that with God we will be victorious.

Look at verse 14: **"So Ahab said, 'By whom?' And he said, 'Thus says the Lord: "By the young leaders of the provinces."' Then he said, 'Who will set the battle in order?' And he answered, 'You'"** (NKJV). Ahab looks at the prophet and asks the question, "Who will lead us to victory?" The prophet answers by saying the young leaders will. Ahab then asks, "Who will set the battle in order?" In other words, he is wondering who will lead the young people out to war. The prophet answers by telling Ahab, "You will." Ahab still does not understand that God is telling him that He is going to bless him with victory. What is God saying to us right now? If we will dare to stand up for God by standing up to the world, God says He's going to empower us to victory.

Look at verse 15: "Then he mustered the young leaders of the provinces, and there were two hundred and thirty-two; and after them he mustered all the people, all the children of Israel—seven thousand" (NKJV). The king puts together his army. His army includes 232 young leaders and seven thousand other people, including children. This number is nothing compared to the great numbers of Ben-Hadad and the thirty-two kings' armies, but God never needs a majority to win a war. God specializes in taking the meek and sometimes the weak and empowering us to major victory.

Look at verses 16–18: **"So they went out at noon. Meanwhile Ben-Hadad and the thirty-two kings helping him were getting drunk at the command post. The young leaders of the provinces went out first. And Ben-Hadad sent out a patrol, and they told him, saying, 'Men coming out of Samaria!' So he said, 'If they have come out for peace, take them alive; and if they have come out for war, take them alive'"** (NKJV). The enemy, because he wants to keep the pretty women and the children for himself, tells his army to take them alive so that they can work for him and he can rape them. That's what the enemy wants to do with our country right now.

Look at verses 19–20: **"Then these young leaders of the provinces went out of the city with the army which followed them. And each one killed his man; so the Syrians fled, and Israel pursued them; and**

Ben-Hadad the king of Syria escaped on a horse with the cavalry" (NKJV). The young warriors and up and fight, so they kill their enemies and send Ben-Hadad running. That's right: because they are willing to stand up and fight, God gives them the victory.

Look at verse 21: **"Then the king of Israel went out and attacked the horses and chariots, and killed the Syrians with a great slaughter"** (NKJV). The king of Israel stands up and fights because of the young people who had been willing to go out on the front line and stand up for their rights. What is God saying to us? There is no enemy we cannot defeat with the help of God. This Liberal government looks too big and powerful for a small Conservative Christian army to be victorious. However, if we are willing to get back to God, back to His morals, His values, and His perfect will, no matter how big the enemy is, we will be victorious.

4

Reprobate America

What we refuse to consider is that there could be a tipping point with God, a point of no return where finally God says, "Enough is enough." There could be a place and time when God will get so fed up with the United States of America that He will take His hand of protection, love, and guidance away. History tells us that God has done this kind of thing before with the very people He loved most, the Israelites.

The Bible tells of such a time and describes just where we are as a country in the eyes of God: **"And He said, 'Go, and tell this people: "Keep on hearing, but do not understand; Keep on seeing, but do not perceive"** (Isaiah 6:9 NKJV). There are two kinds of people reading this book: The first group is made up of people who hear and understand and who see and perceive. Those of us who fit this description are spiritually intact, capable of both hearing and obeying God's word. Then we have the people who hear but don't understand and who see but don't perceive. Verse 9 tells us that no matter what God says, those people are going to just keep doing what they are doing.

When God called me to lead this movement, I was not exactly clear on what He wanted me to say. He cleared the confusion up rather quickly, as He gave me directions through His word. This, verse 10, is what God has sent me to say to America: **"Make the heart of this people dull, And their ears heavy, And shut their eyes; Lest they see with their eyes, And hear with their ears, And understand with their heart, And return**

and be healed." (NKJV) In other words, God knows that His word, through my mouth, will be dull to point that it will put some of you to sleep. God's word has made many Americans' hearts dull, ears heavy, and eyes closed shut to the point where they have no understanding. What we need to see is that this is okay with God right now. He's okay with us not obeying His word. Is it because He does not love us? Of course not. It's because He has loved us with all that He has, and we've still not humbled ourselves to Him. So now God is at the point that He's willing to leave us to our own destruction.

When God told me to share this message with America, I asked Him the same question that the great prophet Isaiah asked: "Then I said, 'Lord, how long?' And He answered: 'Until the cities are laid waste and without inhabitant, The houses are without a man, The land is utterly desolate.'" God said I have to keep preaching this until the walls of the United States of America have fallen down. What you don't understand is that the day of destruction is at hand. We are on the verge of an economic or military disaster that could destroy this country as we know it. We have become a sinful generation to the point that God has turned His back on us. Without His protection, every enemy is now plotting to do what could not have been done when God was our protector.

Because some of you are from the Show Me State, let God show you that the day of the Lord is at hand, and let Him show you why America looks the way it does today. **"The Lord has removed men far away, And the forsaken places *are* many in the midst of the land"** (Isaiah 6:12 NKJV). God is sick and tired of the Untied Sates of America. We have turned our backs on Him to the point that He has now turned His back on us.

Listen to how God describes us in His word: **"Professing to be wise, they became fools, and changed the glory of the incorruptible God into an image made like corruptible man—and birds and four-footed animals and creeping things"** (Romans: 1:22 NKJV). God says we've reduced Him to the likes of a common sinful person. The scripture says, "Professing to be wise, they became fools," meaning we have become a people so smart with business, technology, and philosophical theories, that we've become dumb to the things of God. As a result, we don't fear God and have become a dumb people, without wisdom. God, because He loves us and wants to draw us back to Him, has given us over to our own wills.

Romans 1:24 expands on this idea: **"Therefore God also gave them up to uncleanness, in the lusts of their hearts, to dishonor their bodies among themselves, who exchanged the truth of God for the lie, and worshiped and served the creature rather than the Creator, who is blessed forever. Amen."** (NKJV) God says, essentially, "If you want to live a life without Me, so be it." We have stopped serving Him to start serving each other.

To make sure you understand that God has turned us over to our own wills, let the word speak for itself. **"For this reason God gave them up to vile passions. For even their women exchanged the natural use for what is against nature"** (Romans 1:26 NKJV). Does this look or sound familiar? Women were created to bear children and be virtuous women of God. A woman can't bear a child from another woman. They have moved away from their natural use to that which is unnatural. These women call themselves "lesbians" and are part of the ever-growing gay and lesbian community in this country. This is happening right now. The day of the Lord is at hand.

Look at verse 27: **"Likewise also the men, leaving the natural use of the woman, burned in their lust for one another, men with men committing what is shameful, and receiving in themselves the penalty of their error which was due."** Men are having sex with other men, not desiring a woman—does this look or sound familiar? These men are referred to as "gay" and are part of the ever-growing population of people whom satan is using to destroy the family structure by inserting same sex-marriage into our country. Why would a man want to lie with another man? Let's face it: when God created woman, he created the most beautiful thing ever. What man would rather embrace a hard, rusty, hairy man as opposed to a soft, beautiful woman? Any man who prefers a man over a woman is certifiably sick—sinfully sick, in fact.

Is it possible that the penalty of the gay man's error that verse 27 refers to is AIDS, which was brought into our country mainly through homosexual interactions? This is happening right now. The day of the Lord is at hand!

Look at verse 28: **"And even as they did not like to retain God in their knowledge, God gave them over to a debased mind, to do those things which are not fitting."** (NKJV) God has given us over to all types of sin, including unrighteousness, sexual immorality, wickedness, murder, deceit, evil-mindedness, God-hating, and violence. *Debased* is another word for *reprobate*, which is a word used to describe a no-good sinner or a good-for-nothing wrongdoer. This is the current state of our country. Once the greatest country in history, the United States of America is now relegated to being a godless nation on the way to total destruction.

So if God has turned His back on our country and we are on the way to total and complete destruction, why would I be encouraging God's people, the redeemed of the Lord, to stand up for God in this country? The only reason and the reason I've written this book is found in Scripture: **"But yet a tenth will be in it, And will return and be for consuming, As a terebinth tree or as an oak, Whose stump remains when it is cut down. So the holy seed shall be its stump"** (Isaiah 6:13 NKJV). The holy seed shall be its stump. Jesus is the stump for the 10 percent of Americans who are ready to get back to God. God has sent me for the 10 percent who will hear and obey the word of God. When this country is cut down, God wants to save the stump of righteousness, mercy, grace, and love, the 10 percent who will stand up for God's values, principles, and morals. God wants to save those who are ready to come back to Him.

5

You Sluggard

I have to admit it is very easy to sit back on the sidelines and allow satan to wreak havoc in our country. I know this well simply because for many years I did the same. It's interesting that I did something so horrible while pastoring a church and doing ministry for many years. In my mind, because God called me to be His evangelist and a pastor, my only responsibility was to offer salvation to those people who make up the least, the last, and the lost. I was content preaching the gospel of Jesus Christ from the pulpit Sunday after Sunday and paying little attention to the political issues that were negatively affecting the community around me.

One day something very interesting happened. I got a telephone call from a good friend, Ted Knaak. Ted invited me to go to a meeting with him on a Saturday night. I knew very little of what the meeting was about. It turned out to be Tea Party meeting. I must admit that it was not the type of meeting I would normally sign up for. You see, I'd heard all the ugly stories about the Tea Party. I'd heard from the media that they were racist white people who did not really care about the plight of people of color. Being a black man, as I said, I would not typically sign up for such a meeting.

As fate would have it, when we went inside the meeting room I found about two hundred people, all but one of whom were white. There was one black person: me. The first speaker got up. He encouraged everyone to strengthen our fight against abortion. He explained that more and more abortion clinics were opening all over central Florida. When he was done, I found myself applauding. The second speaker got up. He encouraged everyone to strengthen our fight against government intrusion. He explained how the government was destroying the African-American family structure by continuing to offer welfare as an answer. When he was done speaking, I found myself applauding. The last speaker got up and encouraged everyone to strengthen our fight against the same-sex marriage political agenda. By the time he was done speaking, I was not only applauding but also standing.

Then the unthinkable happened. The facilitator of the meeting announced from the microphone, "We have a pastor from Orlando, Dexter Sanders here with us. Why don't you come up and have a few words?" I was completely unprepared and surprised. Nevertheless, I went to the podium and began to speak.

I found myself speaking from the abundance of the experience I had on the streets of Orlando ministering to the poor. God had blessed our ministry to open transition houses for those folks who were homeless and wanting to improve their lives. God blessed us to run a bus ministry for inner-city children; we bused them out of the inner city every Saturday, feeding them both physical and spiritual food. It was there in the midst of doing the ministry on the street that I found that though we had good hearts, we were using the wrong strategy. We found that handouts did not work. As a matter of fact, not only did we discover that the handouts did not work, we found them to be a hindrance to the very people we said we loved and served.

As I stood at the podium, I thought to myself and said to the people who were sitting there, "Maybe that's the problem with President Obama. Maybe he has a right heart, but is simply using the wrong strategy." He was spending trillions of dollars on handouts for struggling people, especially those in African-American communities; in other words, he was funding the welfare system. I've later come to believe that President Obama neither has the right heart nor the right strategy.

That night God spoke to my heart: "Dexter Sanders, how can you not be concerned with something that I am so concerned about—the plight of the United States of America?" That night the Back 2 God Movement began.

You see, I understand how you can live life thinking you're doing the right things while really doing all the wrong things.

After that experience, I had more time to think about my blindness. I'm a person who God has blessed with education, having received a bachelor's degree and two master's degrees in education. This led me to a key question: if a person as educated as I was who was also a follower of Jesus Christ could be so blind, how many millions of others were suffering the same blindness? God woke me up and instructed me to go into the world and tell His children, the redeemed of the Lord, that it is time to wake up. It's time to get up. It's time to get back to God.

God gave me a scripture that describes the plight of the Conservative Christian people in this country: **"Go to the ant, you sluggard! Consider her ways and be wise, Which, having no captain, Overseer or ruler, Provides her supplies in the summer, And gathers her food in the harvest"** (Proverbs 6:6–8 NKJV). Every time I read this scripture, I can't help but laugh. You would be laughing too if you understood that the sluggard God is referring to in verse six is you. The sluggard in verse six refers to each of the millions of Christians in this country who up until this point have not stood up for God's principles. God says, If you really want to know what it looks like to obey My voice, just check out My ant in verse six.

The scripture says the ant has no overseer or ruler but gets up every day and goes about her duties, doing exactly what God put the ant on the earth to do. No one has to tell the ant when to get up, and no one has to tell the ant when to lie down. The ant does exactly what God instructs her to do and, as a result, verse 8 says the ant **"provides her supplies in the summer and gathers her food in the harvest."** In other words, because the ant is completely obedient to God, she wants for nothing. The ant does not sign up for welfare. The ant does not need a government bailout. The ant does not need government subsidies. The ant is not trillions of dollars in the hole. The ant is a lender, not a borrower. We certainly could learn some lessons from the ant.

Finally, verse 9 gives each of us the question we need to ask ourselves: **"How long will you slumber, O sluggard? When will you rise from your sleep?"** (NKJV) How long will we continue to sleep, Christian Americans? What else needs to happen for you to rise from your sleep? How about another terrorist attack? How about his and his towels in the White House? How about her and her towels in the White House?

What many don't understand is that our country is right on the edge of total destruction. Any day now an economic event could render this nation helpless. A military conflict could bring destruction on United States soil. It's time for us to get back to God's principles and stand up for His rights. It's up us as children of the most high God. It is our voice God is waiting to hear.

Psalm 107:2 says, **"Let the redeemed of the Lord say so, Whom He has redeemed from the hand of the enemy."** (NKJV) The redeemed the Lord have said nothing lately. The redeemed of the Lord have been quiet. Our voices have been silenced of our own choosing. In an attempt to be politically correct, we have remained silent. In an attempt to not offend anyone, the redeemed of the Lord have remained silent. Because of selfish ambitions and motivations, the redeemed of the Lord have remained silent. God says now is the time for the redeemed of the Lord to say so! Say what, one might ask?

Let the redeemed of the Lord stand up and say no to a Liberal government on the fast track to socialism!

Let the redeemed of the Lord stand up and say no to the notion that homosexuality is a normal and acceptable practice in this country!

Let the redeemed of the Lord stand up and say no to same-sex marriage!

That the redeemed of the Lord stand up and say no to murder through abortion!

Let the redeemed of the Lord say no to government intrusion!

Let the redeemed of the Lord say so!

6

Are You Ready for Battle?

I had a conversation with a dear friend recently who told me that while listening to God's directive to get back to God, he could not think of anything else other than how he would be able do it. My first thought was, *Praise the Lord for the fact that it is now in the forefront of his mind!* Later God gave me a message for my friend and for anyone else who may be having similar thoughts. How will God bring us back to Himself?

First, God is calling His people back to Himself collectively, meaning we must be one people. This notion of being one people is so eloquently demonstrated by Jesus Christ himself when he says, **"I do not pray for these alone, but also for those who will believe in Me through their word; that they all may be one, as You, Father, are in Me, and I in You; that they also may be one in Us, that the world may believe that You sent Me"** (John 17:20–21 NKJV). Jesus prayed that we'd be one. The Back 2 God Movement is intended to bring us together as the children of God, to collectively stand up for God. The fight against satan is one that each of us must be willing to engage in.

Second, it's important to know how we will fight satan and stop Him from destroying this country, or at least how we will save God's children from disaster. The Bible encourages us: **"Finally, my brethren, be strong in the Lord and in the power of His might. Put on the whole armor of God, that you may be able to stand against the wiles of the devil"** (Ephesians 6:10–11 NKJV). God suggest in His word that we put on the whole armor of God when the time comes (which is right now) to fight for the rights of God's principles in this country.

Look at the next verse: **"For we do not wrestle against flesh and blood, but against principalities, against powers, against the rulers of the darkness of this age, against spiritual hosts of wickedness in the heavenly places"** (Ephesians 6:12 NKJV). Verse 12 suggest that the fight ahead of us will not be with guns, missiles, and bombs. It will not be a fight to determine what country has the stronger chemical weapons program. Instead our fight is a spiritual fight; it is not against flesh and blood but against principalities and powers that are in darkness and living in spiritual wickedness. This is a very important fact; most people believe battles are against certain sets of people.

The Republicans want to fight the Democrats. The Democrats want to fight the Republicans. The blacks want to fight the whites, and the whites want to fight the blacks. God is trying to make us understand that the battle is not against each other; it's against satan, the one responsible for bringing confusion, division, greed, and pride into our country. Yes, satan has used individuals for his quest, but the spirit that we war against is that of satan himself. God gives us specific instruction on how to battle: **"Therefore take up the whole armor of God, that you may be able to withstand in the evil day, and having done all, to stand. Stand therefore, having girded your waist with truth, having put on the breastplate of righteousness"** (Ephesians 6:13–14 NKJV).

The Girdle of Truth

Verse 14 suggests that we need to gird our waist with truth. The girdle of truth is used to tighten up your spiritual convictions and your walk in Christ. In order to tighten it up, you must be willing to incorporate honesty, sincerity, openness, frankness, and integrity into your spiritual life. When properly wearing your girdle of truth, you will be true to yourself, true to others, and more importantly, true to God Almighty, who already knows your heart. You need to do more than talk the talk; you need to walk the walk.

The Breastplate of Righteousness

Verse 14 also suggests that we should put on a breastplate. The breastplate protects the heart. In Proverbs 4:23 Solomon wrote, **"Above all else, guard your heart, for it affects everything you do." (NKJV)** What you have in your heart determines what you will do with your entire life, be it good or evil. The breastplate of righteousness guards the heart from the infiltration of evil desires by using truth, morality, and justice as a shield.

The Shoes of Preparation

The next verse, verse 15, suggests that our feet need to be prepared: "... and having shod your feet with the preparation of the gospel of peace" (NKJV). Make it possible for you to run for your Lord and Savior Jesus Christ! Your shoes will take you wherever you need to go, as long as they are prepared. How do you ensure that your shoes are prepared? You prepare by studying the word of God, by memorizing scriptures, and by gaining the ability to articulate the message. In order to be to be ready to share the gospel with anyone at anytime and at any place, you have to be prepared.

The Shield of Faith

Verse 16 suggests we need the shield of faith: "... above all, taking the shield of faith with which you will be able to quench all the fiery darts of the wicked one" (NKJV). When satan attacks, be assured that he's coming at the things that will hurt you most. We need to remember that God has our back. The shield of faith serves as both protection and provision for you and anyone else God has given you, be it your wife, husband, children, or church congregation. The shield of faith is used to cover all parts of the body of Christ, whether personal or corporate.

The Helmet of Salvation

Verse 17 tells us to put on a helmet: **"And take the helmet of salvation, and the sword of the Spirit, which is the word of God"** (NKJV). A helmet is used to protect the head, but God's helmet of salvation serves to both protect the head and the mind. As we've already determined, the battlefield is in our minds, so it doesn't take a rocket scientist to figure out the importance of protecting it. Salvation is obtained by confessing and believing Jesus is Lord. When we know this, a helmet is created that protects our mind.

The Sword of the Sprit

Verse 17 also tells us to arm ourselves with the sword. The sword is our transition weapon, simply because it can be used for both defense when we are being attacked and also for offense to destroy the enemy. The sword of the Spirit not only protects us but also thrusts us into a devastating offense attack that renders satan completely defeated.

We now know the weapons that God wants us to use: our girdle of truth, our breastplate of righteousness, our shoes of preparation, our helmet of salvation, and our sword of the spirit. Notice that these weapons cover every major part of the body except the back. Many people familiar with this scripture contend that God has left our backs unprotected. One thing we need to remember is to never look at the scriptures in isolation. We need only to go to Psalm 23 to find the protection God has given us for our backs.

> **The Lord is my shepherd; I shall not want.**
> **He makes me to lie down in green pastures;**
> **He leads me beside the still waters.**
> **He restores my soul;**
> **He leads me in the paths of righteousness**
> **For His name's sake.**
> **Yea, though I walk through the valley of the shadow of death,**
> **I will fear no evil;**
> **For You are with me;**
> **Your rod and Your staff, they comfort me.**
> **You prepare a table before me in the presence of my enemies;**
> **You anoint my head with oil;**
> **My cup runs over.**
> **Surely goodness and mercy shall follow me**
> **All the days of my life;**

**And I will dwell in the house of the Lord
Forever.**

God tells us that He is our shepherd and that we shall never want for anything. He promises to lie us down in green pastures so we can meditate and receive the promises of God. He promises to restore our souls, and He promises to lead us on the path of righteousness for His name's sake. He promises that in the shadow of death He will be there for us, even as our tables are prepared in the presence of our enemies. Finally, in verse 6, He promises that **"goodness and mercy" will follow us all the days of our lives and that forever we "will dwell in the house of the Lord."**

So now let's go through the ways we are protected. Our heads are protected by the helmet of salvation. Our feet are protected by the shoes of preparation. Our hearts are protected by the breastplate of righteousness. We have the shield of faith to protect us from the enemy's arrows of attack. Our waists are protected by the girdle of truth. We also have the sword of the Spirit, of course, and now we have protection for our backs: God promises His goodness and mercy will follow us all the days of our lives.

Now that we have all that we need to fight, it's battle time. Let's check out God's strategy for battle. We can do this by examining history to see if there has ever been a situation similar to the one this country is in right now.

As always, our first source is the Bible: **"It happened after this that the people of Moab with the people of Ammon, and others with them besides the Ammonites, came to battle against Jehoshaphat. Then some came and told Jehoshaphat, saying, 'A great multitude is coming against you from beyond the sea, from Syria; and they are in Hazazon Tamar' (which is En Gedi)"** (2 Chronicles 20:1–2 NKJV). Second Chronicles 20 tells the story of King Jehoshaphat, the king of Judah. He has just been notified that a great army is about to rise up against him and his people.

Look at verse 3: **"And Jehoshaphat feared, and set himself to seek the Lord, and proclaimed a fast throughout all Judah"** (NKJV). The Bible tells us that Jehoshaphat was afraid, but instead of running or consulting the men of this country, he sets himself to seek the Lord. Not only that, but he proclaims a fast throughout all of Judea. One thing is clear: if the United States of America is to stand a chance at once again becoming a great nation and at avoiding destruction, we to must seek the Lord. We have to get to a place where we understand that without God's guidance, we are a lost and defeated people.

Look at verse 4: **"So Judah gathered together to ask help from the Lord; and from all the cities of Judah they came to seek the Lord"** (NKJV). The Bible tells us that not only does Jehoshaphat the leader of Judah seek God, but also all the people in the land do the same. Just imagine what it would look like if all the people of this nation who claim to love the Lord came together from all fifty-two states and sought after God. What an amazing feat that would be—and it is probably nothing short of what is necessary to save our country.

Look at verses 5–6: **"Then Jehoshaphat stood in the assembly of Judah and Jerusalem, in the house of the Lord, before the new court, and said: 'O Lord God of our fathers, are You not God in heaven, and do You not rule over all the kingdoms of the nations, and in Your hand is there not power and might, so that no one is able to withstand You?'"** (NKJV). This is a great moment: Jehoshaphat stands before all the people and begins to talk to God by asking the question. Essentially Jehoshaphat asks, "Are you not God Almighty, the God who holds all power in your hand? Are you not the God that no one stands up against?"

Jehoshaphat continues this line of questioning in verses 7–8: **"Are You not our God, who drove out the inhabitants of this land before Your people Israel, and gave it to the descendants of Abraham Your friend forever? And they dwell in it, and have built You a sanctuary in it for Your name"** (NKJV). Jehoshaphat reminds God that He is the one who originally saved them from the Pharaoh in Egypt. He reminds God that He and His people are the descendants of His friend Abraham. We here in the United States of America need to first repent and ask God's forgiveness. Then we too can remind God that we were at one time the apples of His eye.

Look at verse 8 again as it continues into verse 9: **"And they dwell in it, and have built You a sanctuary in it for Your name, saying, 'If disaster comes upon us—sword, judgment, pestilence, or famine—we will stand before this temple and in Your presence (for Your name is in this temple), and cry out to You in our affliction, and You will hear and save'"** (NKJV). Jehoshaphat could have called on many different military strategies. However, he chooses the one strategy that he knows will allow him and his people to successfully defeat the enemy. Jehoshaphat tells God in verse 9 that they are going to stand with God even if disaster comes upon them. Even if the enemy slaughters them, Jehoshaphat promises to stand before God and cry out. He is confident that God will even then save them. We too need to take the position that come hell or high water we will stand before God, even if it means destruction coming upon our land.

Look at verses 10–11: **"And now, here are the people of Ammon, Moab, and Mount Seir—whom You would not let Israel invade when they came out of the land of Egypt, but they turned from them and did not destroy them—here they are, rewarding us by coming to throw us out of Your possession which You have given us to inherit"** (NKJV). Jehoshaphat begins to reason with God, reminding Him that the enemy could have been destroyed by Israel when Israel was freed from Egypt. For some reason God allowed the enemy to live. Now Jehoshaphat is saying, "The same enemy that you allowed to live is now threatening to kill us in the very land that you gave us."

Isn't it ironic that many people from foreign nations living in this country represent the very people who could bring war against us? The threat of ISIS and the rise of Islam in this nation are unprecedented. Yet the United States of America is the home of many Muslim people. Is it possible that God will allow the very people we house to take over this nation?

Look at verse 12: **"O our God, will You not judge them? For we have no power against this great multitude that is coming against us; nor do we know what to do, but our eyes are upon You"** (NKJV). Jehoshaphat calls on the Lord and asks God to fight this great multitude. He says that he and his people don't know what to do, but nevertheless their eyes will remain steadfast upon the Lord. This too would be great advice for the United States of America. No matter what it looks like, or how bad it sounds, we need to keep our eyes on God.

Look at verse 13: **"Now all Judah, with their little ones, their wives, and their children, stood before the Lord"** (NKJV). As we get ready to go to battle, should we too as a people stand before the Lord? Should we, the church of Jesus Christ, stand before the Lord? I wonder how many people out there in this country are willing to stand with me right now. Who will stand with me?

For those of us who are willing to stand, 2 Chronicles 20:14–25 tells us what we can expect. Look at verse 14, for starters: **"Then the Spirit of the Lord came upon Jahaziel the son of Zechariah, the son of Benaiah, the son of Jeiel, the son of Mattaniah, a Levite of the sons of Asaph, in the midst of the assembly"** (NKJV). Because Judah has faithfully turned its face toward the Lord, the spirit of God comes upon one of its men, Jahaziel. If we turn our face to God and get back to His principles, we too can expect a visitation from the Spirit of the Lord to men and women all across this nation.

Look at verse 15: **"And he said, 'Listen, all you of Judah and you inhabitants of Jerusalem, and you, King Jehoshaphat! Thus says the Lord to you: "Do not be afraid nor dismayed because of this great multitude, for the battle is not yours, but God's"'"** (NKJV). God tells Jahaziel to tell Jehoshaphat and his people to pay no mind to the multitude of people standing before them. He tells them to ignore the threat of war and promises that the battle is not theirs but God's. I believe that if our nation would repent of its sins against God, even though nations will rise up against us, God will step in and fight the battle for us. If we remain disobedient to God, He will allow these countries to destroy us.

Look at verse 16: **"Tomorrow go down against them. They will surely come up by the Ascent of Ziz, and you will find them at the end of the brook before the Wilderness of Jeruel"** (NKJV). In the same way God told David he could go after the enemy, likewise, God is telling the children of Judah that they should go down against the enemy. God is telling you and me right now that it is battle time! It's time to be victorious as individuals and as a nation.

The one thing we must remember is that God does not think the way we think, God does not behave the way we behave, and God certainly does not fight the way we fight. Look at the instruction God gives Judah in verse 17: **"You will not need to fight in this battle. Position yourselves, stand still and see the salvation of the Lord, who is with you, O Judah and Jerusalem! Do not fear or be dismayed; tomorrow go out against them, for the Lord is with you"** (NKJV). God gives Judah and Jerusalem a strategy that I'm sure most of them did not agree with on first sight. I mean, who goes into a battle planning not to fight? God promises them victory if they will merely show up for the battle and watch the mighty hand of God fight for them. I'm trying to imagine our military forces, under the leadership of President Obama, depending on God to fight for America. What a joke! I say that because this current administration would first have to believe in God Almighty, honor His word, and be led by His principles, morals, and values. It's clear to see they are far from that.

Look at 2 Chronicles 20:18–19 to see what happens next in the biblical record: **"And Jehoshaphat bowed his head with his face to the ground, and all Judah and the inhabitants of Jerusalem bowed before the Lord, worshiping the Lord. Then the Levites of the children of the Kohathites and of the children of the Korahites stood up to praise the Lord God of Israel with voices loud and high."** (NKJV) After God promises them victory, the king and all his people stand and begin to worship the Lord God of Israel. The only way our nation can ever expect to experience God's mighty hand as we have in days past is to turn our will back to God, stand before Him, and begin to worship Him.

Look at verse 20: **"So they rose early in the morning and went out into the Wilderness of Tekoa; and as they went out, Jehoshaphat stood and said, 'Hear me, O Judah and you inhabitants of Jerusalem: Believe in the Lord your God, and you shall be established; believe His prophets, and you shall prosper.'"** The United States of America needs a president like Jehoshaphat, one who will stand up and lead us based on the promises of God, not our military strength. In the end, our military will be no match for the forces God will allow to come upon us.

Look at verses 21–22: **"And when he had consulted with the people, he appointed those who should sing to the Lord, and who should praise the beauty of holiness, as they went out before the army and were saying: 'Praise the Lord, For His mercy endures forever.' Now when they began to sing and to praise, the Lord set ambushes against the people of Ammon, Moab, and Mount Seir, who had come against Judah; and they were defeated." (NKJV)** When the people begin to praise the Lord in song, God begins to move! We can learn a lot from these people. It is their praise that activated God's promise. The promise was in place; it needed only a people to step out in faith through obedience, belief, and praise.

We have to get to the point where obedience, belief, and praise are the most important things we do. No amount of economic or military strength can save us. Our only hope is for God to forgive us, come to our aid, and battle for us.

How does God win the battle for Jehoshaphat and the people of Judah? Look at verses 23–25: **"For the people of Ammon and Moab stood up against the inhabitants of Mount Seir to utterly kill and destroy them. And when they had made an end of the inhabitants of Seir, they helped to destroy one another. So when Judah came to a place overlooking the wilderness, they looked toward the multitude; and there were their dead bodies, fallen on the earth. No one had escaped. When Jehoshaphat and his people came to take away their spoil, they found among them an abundance of valuables on the dead bodies, and precious jewelry, which they stripped off for themselves, more than**

they could carry away; and they were three days gathering the spoil because there was so much." God Almighty Himself steps in and fights the battle for the nation of Judah. How then can we get God to continue to fight for us? I say "continue" because the United States of America has never been defeated by another country; God has been with us. Because we have now turned our backs on God, it is conceivable that God will not continue to fight for us. The only way God will continue to fight for us is if we return to Him and stand up for His principles, morals, and values in this country.

7

Time to Get "Turnt" Up

Time to get turnt up! Notice I didn't say, "Time to get turned up." The latter phrase is proper Standard English used by people around my age or older. It is an action; it occurs when you take something in its present state and increase it. For example, if you're baking a turkey and notice that the stove is not hot enough, you have to turn up the heat. The same applies if your house is cold; you might need to turn up the heat.

However, that's not what we're talking about today. After church service on many nights, my sixteen-year-old son, Blake, would frequently walk up to me and say, "Dad, let's get turnt up." Finally I asked him what it meant. He replied that it means you get super excited about something and don't want to calm down unless you have to. My dear son gets super excited about his music and dance and having fun.

Today God wants you to know that it's time to get turnt up. It's time to get so excited about something that we start a party that never ends. The reason God has directed me to speak strongly to Conservative Christian Americans is that God has empowered us—especially you, if you are younger—to take over this country. God says that the older generation has been scared to the point that it won't stand up for God. It has gotten complacent, willing to sit back and let the church and this country go down the drain. But God has sent me to tell you that it's time to get turnt up.

The fact of the matter is, as the Bible says, "**The Spirit of the Lord is upon Me, Because He has anointed Me To preach the gospel to the poor; He has sent Me to heal the brokenhearted, To proclaim liberty to the captives And recovery of sight to the blind, To set at liberty those who are oppressed; To proclaim the acceptable year of the Lord**" (Luke 4:18–19 NKJV). God has sent me, His evangelist, to lead a movement back to God—the Back 2 God Movement! I'm calling Conservative Christians, young and old, to stand with me as we lead this country back to God.

In order for this movement to go forth, God is calling His warriors, the redeemed of the Lord, to the battlefield. There are other people who have not quite surrendered to the gospel that God may use; however, God has designed this battle for you Conservative Christians who are bold and not afraid to stand up for what is right.

People, God says it's time to get turnt up for the Lord, to get excited for the Lord, to start a God party that never ends. It's time to take a world that's upside down with sin and disrespect to God and turn it right side up. Who's ready to go?

Let's go to Scripture, namely Isaiah 35:3–8, to get our marching orders from God.

Verse 3 says, "**Strengthen the weak hands, And make firm the feeble knees**" (NKJV). The weak hands that need to be strengthened are those Christians who have sat back and watched the enemy wreak havoc on our schools, communities, and churches. Adults, you can strengthen the hands of the youth by guiding them, with the word of God, toward spiritual war. Young people, you can strengthen adults' hands by simply standing and being an example of what a warrior for Christ looks like.

Look at verse 4**: "Say to those who are fearful-hearted, 'Be strong, do not fear! Behold, your God will come with vengeance, With the recompense of God; He will come and save you'"** (NKJV). If you can hear God speak through me right now, stand up and tell the people older and younger than you, "Be strong! Do not fear!" We the children of God have been scared to stand up for God for too long! Now is the time to take back what the enemy has stolen. In this same verse, God tells us why we can stand with boldness, and confidence that we will be victorious: **"God will come with vengeance, With the recompense of God; He will come and save you."**

Vengeance means to take revenge or retaliation. *Recompense* means payment or reward. What is God saying to us? God is telling us how He's going to show up! He promises us to show up with a vengeance against satan for the way he has taken this country's people and led them down the path of destruction. God promises to pay back those who would try to exalt themselves against His will.

Look at verse 5: **"Then the eyes of the blind shall be opened, And the ears of the deaf shall be unstopped"** (NKJV). God's people, when you tell your friends and families it's time to go back to God, their blind eyes will be opened and their deaf ears shall be unstopped. They will join in the fight against all unrighteousness in our country. They will stand with us as we take back our schools. They will stand with us as we take back our communities. They will stand with us as we take back our families. They will even stand with us as we take back our government.

Look at verse 6: **"Then the lame shall leap like a deer, And the tongue of the dumb sing. For waters shall burst forth in the wilderness, And streams in the desert"** (NKJV). When we tell those around us it's time to get back to God, "the lame shall leap like a deer." The lame are the Christians who have been sitting on the sidelines doing nothing as our country goes down the drain. God says when we stand up, they will leap into action like the deer. This verse also says, **"And the tongue of the dumb sing."** The dumb are those Christians who have been silent as the enemy has literally destroyed our country. God says when we stand up, they will lift their voices to take a stand for God's morals and values in this country.

Then the verse tells us that **"the lame shall leap like a deer, And the tongue of the dumb sing. For waters shall burst forth in the wilderness,**

And streams in the desert." The wilderness and the desert represent the church and our country. Both are dry and dead, but when we stand up and invite this community, this city, and this country back to God, God says His spiritual living water shall burst forth in the church and in this country like never before.

Look at verse 7: **"The parched ground shall become a pool, And the thirsty land springs of water; In the habitation of jackals, where each lay, There shall be grass with reeds and rushes"** (NKJV). Again, the parched ground and thirsty land are the so-called people of God who are "lame" and "dumb," and it also refers to their country. God says this dried up and sinful place shall become green with life because of the work that you, the Conservative Christian nation, are about to do.

Look at verse 8: **"A highway shall be there, and a road, And it shall be called the Highway of Holiness. The unclean shall not pass over it, But it shall be for others. Whoever walks the road, although a fool, Shall not go astray"** (NKJV). The work that you will do through this Back 2 God movement will allow people the opportunity to walk down the highway of holiness and commune with our God in the way He designed for us. Even though we have made foolish mistakes in the past, our commitment to get back to God and serve Him in this country will allow us to walk the road of victory with our Lord and Savior Jesus Christ. It's time to get turnt up for God!

8

Take It Back

The Bible tells us that God blessed King Ahab and his people to eventually be victorious even though Ahab had been afraid to stand up against the enemy. This victory was accomplished without him or Israel losing anything—except maybe a little pride. Unlike King Ahab and the nation of Israel, our current situation in the United States of America suggests that we have lost many things. To date we have lost the economic, military, social, and spiritual edge we once enjoyed as the dominant force in the world. God wants to suggest to us today that if we are willing to get back to God, God will return to us and continue to love this country and cause it to prosper as in the days of old. God also wants us to understand that not only will He prosper us for the future, but he also will return to us everything that we lost at the hands of the enemy.

One might ask why God would restore the United States of America and everything it lost. The answer is simple: that's just the way God is. As Christians in this nation, under God, we can count on a God who is forgiving and willing to continue to love us unconditionally. The notion that God will restore to us everything that we've lost to the enemy is not new. This is something that has happened time and time again with the Israelites, God's chosen people. Similarly, God is ready to empower the United States of America to take back what the enemy has stolen from us.

On a personal level, how many of you have fallen victim to the thief? I didn't say *a* thief but *the* thief. I mean the thief the Bible refers to when it says, "He comes to kill, steal and destroy." Have you fallen victim to the thief? What has he taken from you? Has he taken any of your loved ones while they were still living in sin? Has he taken any of your dreams? What has this evil, no good, lying, cheating, stealing, thieving enemy taken from you?

God sent me to tell you that whatever the enemy has taken from you, you ought to take it back. Now, I know you can't get the dead back, but you can make sure their living was not in vain by learning from their plights and never allowing satan to reign in your life or the lives of your family, friends, or country.

You can take back the dreams God gave you. You can take back the visions God gave you. You can, even now, stand up and be the woman or man of God He meant for you to be. God sent me to tell you that you have to take it back.

God wants to show you two things: First, you have a right to go after what has been taken from you. Second, God wants to tell you how to do it. Let's take a look at 1 Samuel 30:1–18, verses that demonstrates God's willingness to return to us what has been lost to the enemy. They will help us understand what God has in store for us.

Here are verses 1–3: **"Now it happened, when David and his men came to Ziklag, on the third day, that the Amalekites had invaded the South and Ziklag, attacked Ziklag and burned it with fire, and had taken captive the women and those who were there, from small to great; they did not kill anyone, but carried them away and went their way. So David and his men came to the city, and there it was, burned with fire; and their wives, their sons, and their daughters had been taken captive." (NKJV)** In these verses, David is now the King of Israel. As he and his men come into the city, they find that the city has been burned and that their wives, sons, and daughters have been taken captive. One can only imagine the pain and anguish David and the rest of his men feel as they discover that their loved ones have been taken away.

Look at verse 4: **"Then David and the people who were with him lifted up their voices and wept, until they had no more power to weep."** (NKJV) After seeing what they lost, David and his men wept until they could no longer weep. I wonder if we have any people who are weeping for our nations. Even on a personal level, what have you been crying about so hard that you have no power left with which to cry further? God sent me to tell you that maybe it's time to stop crying, get up, and take it back.

Look at verse 5**: "And David's two wives, Ahinoam the Jezreelitess, and Abigail the widow of Nabal the Carmelite, had been taken captive."** David discovers that his prize possessions, his two wives, are gone. The enemy took the most precious things that belonged to him. Such is the case in this country. Satan has used our Liberal government to spearhead a socialist movement that takes away the very liberty this country was founded on. To again turn to the personal level, has the enemy ever taken your spouse, child, or family member? Has he taken this person with drugs, alcohol, or greed? If that is the case, it's time to take him or her back.

Look at verse 6: **"Now David was greatly distressed, for the people spoke of stoning him, because the soul of all the people was grieved, every man for his sons and his daughters. But David strengthened himself in the Lord his God."** Two things happen in this verse. First, David is greatly distressed because everyone around him was grieved. Second, notice what David does about it: "But David strengthened himself in the Lord his God." If ever there was a time for us, the redeemed of the Lord, to strengthen ourselves, it's right now. Now is the time for us to band together as the people of God and take back what the enemy has taken from us, even if we allowed it to happen.

Look at verse 7: **"Then David said to Abiathar the priest, Ahimelech's son, 'Please bring the ephod here to me.' And Abiathar brought the ephod to David."** An ephod was like an apron that had two shoulder straps and attachments with ornaments; it was used to secure a high priest's breastplate, which was worn to protect the chest when engaged in battle. Because, in this verse, the enemy has taken David's family, he puts on his ephod in preparation for going to battle against the enemy who stole from him. It's time for the United States of America to put its ephod on and prepare itself for a spiritual war against the forces of evil. Remember, in David's time the ephod was worn by the high priest. The high priest is a man of God who has been called by God to direct and lead the people. The only way the United States can put on the ephod is to first get back to God and recommit in humility and reverence to the God of Abraham, Isaac, and Jacob. When we come back to God, we can then walk in the priestly authority God gave us when He first blessed this nation.

Look at verse 8: **"So David inquired of the Lord, saying, 'Shall I pursue this troop? Shall I overtake them?' And He answered him, 'Pursue, for you shall surely overtake them and without fail recover all.'"** (NKJV) The same thing applies to our country and to us as individuals. David is mourning the loss of his family. He's also feeling the pressure of the nation, as they are considering stoning him for the loss of their families. In the midst of it all, David steps up and puts his ephod on, but before going any further he stops and inquires of the Lord. He asks God, **"Shall I pursue this troop? Shall I overtake them?"** You see, David has a heart after God. He understands the necessity to include God in every decision of his life. He has grown to understand that he can trust God, especially in the most difficult situations.

We, the United States of America, can learn a lot from King David. So far, we've learned to trust in everything except for God. We've trusted our economic decisions. Just look where that's gotten us: trillions of dollars in the hole. We've trusted our social discernment, but what has that given us? It's given us communities invested with drugs, alcohol, prostitution, greed, and welfare. We've trusted our spiritual understanding, and what has that given us? It's given us a world on a sinful downward spiral through the likes of pornography, obscenity, vulgarity, and homosexuality.

Notice that God promises David victory. Not only does God say David will be victorious, but He also promises that without fail David shall recover everything that he lost! This is a scripture of hope for the United States of America. This verse is a witness to God's desire for us not to only be victorious against our present foe but also to be restored. God promises those of us who love Him that He will restore everything that the enemy has taken away from us.

Look at verses 9–10: **"So David went, he and the six hundred men who were with him, and came to the Brook Besor, where those stayed who were left behind. But David pursued, he and four hundred men; for two hundred stayed behind, who were so weary that they could not cross the Brook Besor."** Notice that David did not go into the fight alone; he took some warriors with him. What is God trying to say to us? Don't take your behind into a fight with satan alone. Take God's warriors with you. That is why it is so essential that we gather together as the redeemed of the Lord. The only way we can defeat satan is to come together as the saints of God. This, however, is not a small feat. Satan has been very successful at driving into our homes, communities, churches, and schools the issues that separate the body of Christ.

Look at verses 11–13. **"Then they found an Egyptian in the field, and brought him to David; and they gave him bread and he ate, and they let him drink water. And they gave him a piece of a cake of figs and two clusters of raisins. So when he had eaten, his strength came back to him; for he had eaten no bread nor drunk water for three days. Then David said to him, "To whom do you belong, and where are you from?" And he said, "I am a young man from Egypt, servant of an Amalekite; and my master left me behind, because three days ago I fell sick." (NKJV)**

This young man worked for the enemy, but when the enemy didn't need him anymore because the young man got sick, the enemy threw him away. God sent me to tell you not to expect the enemy to do any different with you or me or our loved ones. It's certainly no different with our country. Satan is on a mission to destroy us. Once he's done that, he will have no further use of us. That's why it's so important that we remember the fight is against satan, not the human beings he uses as pawns. It's so important that we continue to love our brothers and sisters, despite how they are being used by the enemy. This is especially true as it pertains to our brothers and sisters who are practicing homosexuality. Let us be vigilant against the spirit of darkness, but let us show love to our brother and sisters.

Look at verse 14, as the young Egyptian man keeps talking: **"We made an invasion of the southern area of the Cherethites, in the territory which belongs to Judah, and of the southern area of Caleb; and we burned Ziklag with fire."** As David continues to talk to the young man, he discovers that it was this young man's army that invaded and stole David's wives and family! God brings to the feet of David a man who belongs to the very army that brought him anguish and pain. What's important is the way we handle the enemy. Yes, God calls for us to defeat him at every turn. However, God also calls for us to be "wise as a serpent, yet gentle as a dove."

Let's see how David handles this in verse 15: **"And David said to him, 'Can you take me down to this troop?' So he said, 'Swear to me by God that you will neither kill me nor deliver me into the hands of my master, and I will take you down to this troop.'"** Now God is using for good the same person that satan used for harm. We too have to be open to our brothers and sisters who were once slaves to satan; they too can be used by God for good.

Look at verse 16: **"And when he had brought him down, there they were, spread out over all the land, eating and drinking and dancing, because of all the great spoil which they had taken from the land of the Philistines and from the land of Judah."** (NKJV) Here is the reason you ought to get pissed off. The enemy is kicking back, having a drink, and laughing at you and me right now. He feels secure in his victory, because he believes we could never set aside our selfish ambitions and motivations for the good of this country. The enemy is secure in his belief that we could never come together on one accord. Satan is so sure that we, the redeemed of the Lord, could never love each other the way Christ loves us, so he sits back with a drink in his hand and laughs at us. If you're going to get mad, get mad at that!

David does not allow his anger to affect how he deals with the enemy. He simply grabs his composure and does the will of God. Look at verse

17: **"Then David attacked them from twilight until the evening of the next day. Not a man of them escaped, except four hundred young men who rode on camels and fled."** David attacked the enemy, which is the exact thing God will have us do. We should no longer assume the position of response; instead we should do exactly what David did: attack! However, we should attack not with swords or guns but with the word of the Lord. We should attack by opening our mouths and proclaiming what the Lord says.

Look at verses 18–19: **"So David recovered all that the Amalekites had carried away, and David rescued his two wives. And nothing of theirs was lacking, either small or great, sons or daughters, spoil or anything which they had taken from them; David recovered all."** (NKJV) The Bible says that David recovered all that was taken from him. Is it reasonable to believe that what God did for David and the nation of Israel He'll do for the United States of America? Is it reasonable to believe that God would do that for each of us in our individual lives? If I were a betting man, or if I were *still* a betting man, I would bet that God can and will come to our rescue the same way He did for King David. In fact, I would bet that God would do even more.

Look at verse 20: **"Then David took all the flocks and herds they had driven before those other livestock, and said, 'This is David's spoil.'"** Not only did God restore everything that was taken from David, but He also gave David the spoils of the enemy. What does that mean for our country? What does that mean for you and me? If we turn our lives and our wills over to God and just get back to His morals and values, God is ready to restore everything that we've lost, as well as bless us with the proceeds of the very enemy who came against us. It's time to take it all back!

9

Your Behind Is Mine

The title of this chapter is not an original thought of mine. Instead it came from my mother. When I was a child growing up in Rochester, New York, like other kids I sometimes got into a little mischief. Okay, let me just be honest: I got into a lot of mischief. My mother would warn me time and again that if I continued to do things that she told me not to do, there would be consequences. What that meant was she would punish me in some way or whip my behind. In the worst case scenario, she would simply say, "Wait until your father gets home." Those words alone would turn my world upside down.

When she decided to handle the discipline herself, having concluded that it was time to give me that whipping, she would say, "Dexter DeWayne Sanders, your behind is mine." That meant that she was going to be the deliverer of some major pain to my butt. "Your behind is mine" simply means that a decision has been made to deliver consequences to someone for behavior he or she is responsible for.

In chapter 3 we took a look at the king who was acting like a punk, King Ahab, the leader of the Israelites. We also got a chance to look at a chosen generation of young people who came to the rescue of the scared king. Because they refused to allow the enemy to take anything from them, they were victorious. Let's return to the story of King Ahab in battle with his enemy, Ben-Hadad. Only this time, note King Ahab's different attitude, an attitude that tells the enemy, "Your behind is mine." Let's take a look at Scripture: **"And the prophet came to the king of Israel and said to him, 'Go, strengthen yourself; take note, and see what you should do, for in the spring of the year the king of Syria will come up against you'"** (1 Kings 20:22 NKJV). God comes to King Ahab and warns him that the battle is not over. He essentially says to King Ahab, "Yes, you celebrated victory earlier, but the same enemy is going to come back to try and destroy you."

Look at verse 23 from this same chapter: **"Then the servants of the king of Syria said to him, 'Their gods are gods of the hills. Therefore they were stronger than we; but if we fight against them in the plain, surely we will be stronger than they'"** (NKJV). Ben-Hadad's servants tell him that the only way Israel's army beat them the first time was that they were fighting in hills. In other words, if they had fought any place else, they would have won. Likewise, the enemy of our souls and the enemy of this country knows that the only way we are able to defeat him is when we fight as children of the most high God. Knowing this, his strategy is to move us away from the things of God so that he will have a greater chance of defeating us.

Look at verses 24–25: "'**So do this thing: Dismiss the kings, each from his position, and put captains in their places; and you shall muster an army like the army that you have lost, horse for horse and chariot for chariot. Then we will fight against them in the plain; surely we will be stronger than they.' And he listened to their voice and did so"** (NKJV). The king of Syria listens to his servants as they talk him into fighting God's children on what they believe to be their territory so that he will be victorious this time.

Look at verses 26–28. **"So it was, in the spring of the year, that Ben-Hadad mustered the Syrians and went up to Aphek to fight against Israel. And the children of Israel were mustered and given provisions, and they went against them. Now the children of Israel encamped before them like two little flocks of goats, while the Syrians filled the countryside. Then a man of God came and spoke to the king of Israel, and said, "Thus says the Lord: 'Because the Syrians have said, "The**

Lord is God of the hills, but He is not God of the valleys," therefore I will deliver all this great multitude into your hand, and you shall know that I am the Lord.'" (NKJV)

Once again, just as the battle begins, God sends a messenger to give the king of Israel instructions. This is also happening today. God is sending messengers just like me to give Americans instructions. God's instruction that we need to get back to Him or else we will suffer the consequences.

Look at verse 29: **"And they encamped opposite each other for seven days. So it was that on the seventh day the battle was joined; and the children of Israel killed one hundred thousand foot soldiers of the Syrians in one day"** (NKJV). This time King Ahab is not afraid. This time he stands up for God, and as a result, his army kills one hundred thousand soldiers. The king in essence tells the enemy, "Your behind is mine no matter where we fight, because the Lord God is on our side." This is the same message God has for the United States America: "if you come back to Me, I will continue to fight your battles, and as long as I fight your battles you will never lose. However, if you persist in your disrespectful disobedience to Me, I will allow the enemy to destroy you."

Look at verse 30: **"But the rest fled to Aphek, into the city; then a wall fell on twenty-seven thousand of the men who were left. And Ben-Hadad fled and went into the city, into an inner chamber"** (NKJV). With God on its side Israel could say, "Your behind is mine no matter where you go: in a field, on a hill, or behind a wall." The same is true for us, as it is for this nation. If God is for us, who could be against us?

10

This Is a Job for God

Back in the day, Marvel comics were popular: the major superheroes in comics and on television were Batman and Robin, Aquaman, the Fantastic Four, Wonder Woman, and Superman. Whenever there was a villain so terrible and destructive that the whole world was in danger, you'd hear the announcer on television say, "This is a job for Superman." What that meant was there was no one else who could handle that particular job. The villain was so strong and powerful that no one could stop him—no one, that is, except for Superman, a man bigger and stronger than anyone.

Back in the real world, it's pretty much the same way. Let's say we get to a point where we understand things have gotten so bad that there is no way we can handle them and that there is no way they can be reversed. When we see for ourselves that destruction is surely on the way, those of us who have even the slightest bit of wisdom realize that if we don't get help fast, we are going to die. We understand that the job is no ordinary job. We've tired everything: drugs can't fix it, and money won't make it go away. This is a job for God. It's out of our hands.

God would have me suggest that we are in such a situation right now. This world of ours has been turned upside down and inside out with sin. For some of us, our personal lives have been too.

God would also have me to tell you that nothing is too big for Him. He is sitting high and looking low. Those of us who are trampled by the world need to take refuge in the fact that God will not sit back and allow His faithful few to be destroyed. This is a job for God.

To help us better understand this, let's go to Scripture. Psalm 12:1 says, **"Help, Lord, for the godly man ceases! For the faithful disappear from among the sons of men"** (NKJV).

Things are so bad that there are not many, if any, godly men left. The Bible says the faithful men and women have disappeared from the earth. Doesn't that sound familiar? Today we are hard pressed to find faithful Christian men and women. There was a time when good, strong, God-fearing men stood in pulpits across this nation. However, today many of the pastors and leaders of the so-called church of Jesus Christ have fallen into the grasp of satan himself. Many of them have grown content with preaching a watered down version of the gospel for the sake of appeasing their members, and many of them have started hanging on to their tithes and offerings.

Look at verse 2 of Psalm 12: "**They speak idly everyone with his neighbor; With flattering lips and a double heart they speak"** (NKJV). According to this scripture we have become a people who speak idly. We speak loudly but say nothing, because our talk is absent of God. We just talk about things of the world. Does this sound familiar? We have become a society inundated with negative information by the radio, the television, our movie theaters, and especially the Internet. This information has guided us into conversations that are mute and godless.

That same verse says we speak with flattering lips and double hearts, which means we are a two-faced people. We say one thing but mean another, only looking out for what's best for ourselves with no thought of God.

Look at verse 3: **"May the Lord cut off all flattering lips, And the tongue that speaks proud things"** (NKJV). The writer of this psalm says a prayer, a prayer that I particularly like. He prays, "Lord cut off all their flattering lips." Then he goes on to say the Lord should cut off the tongue that speaks proud things. In other words, he prays God will silence the words and conversation of satan; satan's words emerge from the mouths of millions of Americans.

Look at verse 4: **"Who have said, 'With our tongue we will prevail; Our lips are our own; Who is lord over us?'"** (NKJV). People say they are in control of their own lives. Our country's full of such individuals who believe they do not have to answer to God Almighty. Proud people believe there is no God who lords over us.

Finally we hear God's response to all of this madness. We hear what God Almighty will do to the proud in verse 5: **"'For the oppression of the poor, for the sighing of the needy, Now I will arise,' says the Lord; 'I will set him in the safety for which he yearns'"** (NKJV). God says that He will rise for those of us who are oppressed by the world. God says He will rise for those of us who will stand up for His principles, His morals, and His values.

You need to know that our God is both able and willing to deliver us out of every situation. There is nothing too big for God. He has delivered us, is delivering us right now, and will continue to deliver us from every evil thing. How do I know? Listen to the apostle Paul in 2 Corinthians 1:9: **"Yes, we had the sentence of death in ourselves, that we should not trust in ourselves but in God who raises the dead"** (NKJV). In this verse, Paul is in Asia in a life or death situation. Things are so bad that he says we can no longer trust in ourselves. Instead we have to trust in God, who has the power to raise the dead. We are in the same situation right now. It's life or death—that is, the life or death of the United States of America.

Then Paul goes on to testify about God's power to deliver. God, he says, **"delivered us from so great a death, and does deliver us; in [Him] we trust that He will still deliver us"** (2 Corinthians 1:10 NKJV). Paul says God already did it, God is doing it right now, and God will continue to do it. Do what? Let's break it down:

God already saved you, even while you were yet in your sins. God is delivering you and loving on you right now in your present state, even if you're still all messed up. God will continue to love, empower, and deliver you.

God promises to do these things for us as individuals. However, the same is true for this country. God is willing to continue to love, empower, and deliver the United States of America from its present condition. God is simply looking for a few good men and women who don't count it robbery to stand up for Him. We have become a people so concerned with money and fame that we have no time left for God. Some of us are not completely convinced that it's okay to not be rich, popular, or powerful by the world's standards.

We still spend a great deal of time trying to be like the Joneses next door. We need a lot of money to feel important, we need a big house to feel accomplished, and we need to be in the in crowd to feel successful. God wants me to tell you not to go that way, because that way takes you further and further away from God. He loves you so much and has but one desire: to draw you back to Him.

11

The Josiah Generation

The notion that the United States of America needs to get back to God may be new to this country, but it's not new to history. The fact is that I know we are able as a nation to turn back to God because it has been proven possible before. Time and time again in Scripture we find God's chosen people, the Israelites, turning their backs on God. God then allows them to suffer defeat and humiliation before God comes in and recues His people.

Our country needs godly leadership from the president of the United States all the way down to local political leaders. It's leadership that makes the difference. Whenever God has been able to draw His people back to Himself, there has always been a godly leader in place to direct the people. Such was the case for the nation of Judah under the leadership of King Josiah. During his time, this young king led his own version of our Back 2 God Movement. Maybe by looking at the life of Josiah, we can learn what it takes to get back to God.

Let's go to 2 Kings 22–23, starting with the first two verses of chapter 22: **"Josiah was eight years old when he became king, and he reigned thirty-one years in Jerusalem. His mother's name was Jedidah the daughter of Adaiah of Bozkath. And he did what was right in the sight of the Lord, and walked in all the ways of his father David; he did not turn aside to the right hand or to the left."** (NKJV) Scripture tells us that Josiah came into his reign as king when he was only eight years old.

We also see that he is a man of God. As verse 2 says, **"And he did what was right in the sight of the Lord." (NKJV)**

Let's look at verses 3–7: **"Now it came to pass, in the eighteenth year of King Josiah, that the king sent Shaphan the scribe, the son of Azaliah, the son of Meshullam, to the house of the Lord, saying: "Go up to Hilkiah the high priest, that he may count the money which has been brought into the house of the Lord, which the doorkeepers have gathered from the people. And let them deliver it into the hand of those doing the work, who are the overseers in the house of the Lord; let them give it to those who are in the house of the Lord doing the work, to repair the damages of the house—to carpenters and builders and masons—and to buy timber and hewn stone to repair the house. However there need be no accounting made with them of the money delivered into their hand, because they deal faithfully." (NKJV)**

Josiah sends his men to Hilkiah, the high priest, to do some housekeeping. They are told to give the money that had been collected to the people in the house of the Lord who have been repairing the house.

Look at verse 8: **"Then Hilkiah the high priest said to Shaphan the scribe, 'I have found the Book of the Law in the house of the Lord.' And Hilkiah gave the book to Shaphan, and he read it."** In this verse something very interesting happens. Apparently Hilkiah finds the "Book of the Law." We're talking about the Torah, the five original books of the Bible—Genesis, Exodus, Leviticus, Numbers, and Deuteronomy. The Torah is our original Bible, and for some reason it had not been available to Hilkiah or, more importantly, to Josiah, the king of Judah. Hilkiah gives the Torah to Shaphan the scribe, who then reads it for himself.

Look at verses 9–10: **"So Shaphan the scribe went to the king, bringing the king word, saying, 'Your servants have gathered the money that was found in the house, and have delivered it into the hand of those who do the work, who oversee the house of the Lord.' Then Shaphan the scribe showed the king, saying, 'Hilkiah the priest has given me a book.' And Shaphan read it before the king."** The scribe reports back to Josiah about all that happened, especially finding the book. Shaphan then reads the word of God to the king.

Look at verses 11–13: **"Now it happened, when the king heard the words of the of the Law, that he tore his clothes. Then the king commanded Hilkiah the priest, Ahikam the son of Shaphan, Achbor the son of Michaiah, Shaphan the scribe, and Asaiah a servant of the king, saying, "Go, inquire of the Lord for me, for the people and for all Judah, concerning the words of this book that has been found; for great is the wrath of the Lord that is aroused against us, because our fathers have not obeyed the words of this book, to do according to all that is written concerning us."** (NKJV)

When the king heard the words of God, he tore his clothes as a form of repentance. He then ordered his men to go and inquire of the Lord concerning the words found in the book. Josiah was now concerned that his forefathers had not obeyed the words of God and that God's anger and wrath were aroused against the nation Judah.

Here in the United States of America we are not absent the word of God, but we certainly have failed to obey it. We don't have leaders who are concerned about our disobedience to God and the consequences thereof. Instead, we have leaders, beginning with President Obama, who are hell-bent on creating, enforcing, and/or supporting laws that go against the very nature of God. Our country needs new leadership from godly men and women who not only value the word of God but are also not afraid to stand up for it.

Look at verses 14–17: **"So Hilkiah the priest, Ahikam, Achbor, Shaphan, and Asaiah went to Huldah the prophetess, the wife of Shallum the son of Tikvah, the son of Harhas, keeper of the wardrobe. (She dwelt in Jerusalem in the Second Quarter.) And they spoke with her. Then she said to them, "Thus says the Lord God of Israel, 'Tell the man who sent you to Me, "Thus says the Lord: 'Behold, I will bring calamity on this place and on its inhabitants—all the words of the book which the king of Judah has read—because they have forsaken Me and burned incense to other gods, that they might provoke Me to anger with all**

the works of their hands. Therefore My wrath shall be aroused against this place and shall not be quenched." (NKJV)

Josiah's men go to see the prophetess so they can understand what the word of God is saying to them. When they arrive, the prophetess tells them plainly what is going to happen: She tells them that God is going to bring calamity on the nation of Judah because they turned their backs on the true and living God to serve other gods. This is exactly the same thing our country has done. We have turned our backs on God to serve each other's lustful desires. It's more important in this country to please each other and ourselves than it is to please God. For that reason, as with the nation of Judah, God will allow calamity to come upon us like we've never seen before.

Look at verses 18–20. **"But as for the king of Judah, who sent you to inquire of the Lord, in this manner you shall speak to him, 'Thus says the Lord God of Israel: "Concerning the words which you have heard—because your heart was tender, and you humbled yourself before the Lord when you heard what I spoke against this place and against its inhabitants, that they would become a desolation and a curse, and you tore your clothes and wept before Me, I also have heard you," says the Lord. "Surely, therefore, I will gather you to your fathers, and you shall be gathered to your grave in peace; and your eyes shall not see all the calamity which I will bring on this place."'" So they brought back word to the king." (NKJV)**

The prophetess goes on to tell the men what will happen to Josiah. She explains that because of his tender heart and his willingness to repent and cry out to God, he and his family will be spared. Their eyes will not see the destruction of Judah and they will die peaceful deaths. God spares the life of Josiah and his family because they had been willing to repent and turn back to God.

What does this tell us concerning the United States of America? First, this nation's doom is inevitable because our sins against God are too great. However, as in the days of Josiah, God will save the remnant of His people who repent with humility and turn their wills and their lives back to God.

So far in this story we've learned how Josiah was saved from calamity, even as the nation of Judah would be destroyed, but we have not witnessed him leading anything like our Back 2 God Movement. Let's look at a little more Scripture.

Second Kings 23:1–2 says, **"Now the king sent them to gather all the elders of Judah and Jerusalem to him. The king went up to the house of the Lord with all the men of Judah, and with him all the inhabitants of Jerusalem—the priests and the prophets and all the people, both small and great. And he read in their hearing all the words of the Book of the Covenant which had been found in the house of the Lord."** (NKJV) After hearing that Judah is going to be destroyed but that he and his family are going to be saved, Josiah could simply say, "I'm good; too bad for Judah." But because he is a true man of God, he does not do that. Instead he does not stop trying to save his country. He pulls all the people together and reads the word of God to them. Could you just imagine what this nation would look like if we had a president who respected the word of God and the power thereof such that he would read it to all Americans?

Look at verse 3: **"Then the king stood by a pillar and made a covenant before the Lord, to follow the Lord and to keep His commandments and His testimonies and His statutes, with all his heart and all his soul, to perform the words of this covenant that were written in this book. And all the people took a stand for the covenant."** (NKJV) Josiah stands before the people and makes a commitment to God to follow Him with all his heart, mind, and soul. As a result, all of his people do the same. That just goes to show what a powerful nation we could be with the right godly leadership. Josiah doesn't stop there.

Look at verse 4: **"And the king commanded Hilkiah the high priest, the priests of the second order, and the doorkeepers, to bring out of the temple of the Lord all the articles that were made for Baal, for Asherah, and for all the host of heaven; and he burned them outside Jerusalem in the fields of Kidron, and carried their ashes to Bethel." Then Josiah commands that all articles made to honor other gods (Baal, Asherah, etc.) be burned." (NKJV)** Josiah is still not done.

Look at verse 5: **"Then he removed the idolatrous priests whom the kings of Judah had ordained to burn incense on the high places in the cities of Judah and in the places all around Jerusalem, and those who burned incense to Baal, to the sun, to the moon, to the constellations, and to all the host of heaven."** (NKJV) Josiah then removes the priests who had been responsible for Judah serving other gods. Josiah is still not done. He goes on to remove from the city everything and every person who has gone against the word of God. Not only this, but he also restores and reestablishes God's commands.

Look at verses 21–23: **"Then the king commanded all the people, saying, 'Keep the Passover to the Lord your God, as it is written in this Book of the Covenant.' Such a Passover surely had never been held since the days of the judges who judged Israel, nor in all the days of the kings of Israel and the kings of Judah. But in the eighteenth year of King Josiah this Passover was held before the Lord in Jerusalem."** As it turns out, Judah has not celebrated Passover in many, many years, during which time they have allowed themselves to move further and further from the things of God. Josiah becomes the king who leads his people back to God, just as our Back 2 God Movement intends to do. However, his actions still do not erase the judgment on the people of Judah for turning their backs on God.

Look at verses 26–27: **"Nevertheless the Lord did not turn from the fierceness of His great wrath, with which His anger was aroused against Judah, because of all the provocations with which Manasseh had provoked Him. And the Lord said, 'I will also remove Judah from My sight, as I have removed Israel, and will cast off this city Jerusalem which I have chosen, and the house of which I said, "My name shall be there." (NKJV)** If God would destroy His own holy city, then surely God plans to keep His word about the destruction of any country that refuses to honor Him as God. History tells us that Josiah led his version of what we are calling the Back 2 God Movement, and God is looking for you and me to do the same.

12

The United States of America's Present and Future

Jeremiah 1 begins with these verses: **"The words of Jeremiah the son of Hilkiah, of the priests who were in Anathoth in the land of Benjamin, to whom the word of the Lord came in the days of Josiah the son of Amon, king of Judah, in the thirteenth year of his reign. It came also in the days of Jehoiakim the son of Josiah, king of Judah, until the end of the eleventh year of Zedekiah the son of** Josiah, king of Judah, until the carrying away of Jerusalem captive in the fifth **month"** (Jeremiah 1:1–3 NKJV). Verses 1–3 discuss God bringing the word to the prophet Jeremiah. Today God has brought His word to you and me, those of us willing to stand up and fight for God. This is making very plain our responsibility to stand up for Him in this nation. He also makes very clear the consequences that await a disobedient people.

Look at verses 4–5: **"Then the word of the Lord came to me, saying: 'Before I formed you in the womb I knew you; Before you were born I sanctified you: I ordained you a prophet to the nations'"** (NKJV). These verses speak to those of us who have been called to stand up for God. In short, God is telling us that before we were formed in our mother's wombs He knew that we'd be the ones ready to stand up and go to war. God says to us, the Back 2 God warriors, "Before your name was uttered I called you for such a time as this."

Look at verses 6–7: "**Then said I: 'Ah, Lord God! Behold, I cannot speak, for I am a youth.' But the Lord said to me: 'Do not say, "I am a youth," For you shall go to all to whom I send you, And whatever I command you, you shall speak'**" (NKJV). Because we, the redeemed of the Lord, are few in number, young in our commitment to fight, and without major resources, it seems impossible for us to be used by God to speak to the nation, but God says, "Don't say that! You will go where I tell you to go, do what I tell you to do, and say what I tell you to say."

Look at verses 8–10: "**'Do not be afraid of their faces, For I am with you to deliver you,' says the Lord. Then the Lord put forth His hand and touched my mouth, and the Lord said to me: 'Behold, I have put My words in your mouth. See, I have this day set you over the nations and over the kingdoms, To root out and to pull down, To destroy and to throw down, To build and to plant'**" (NKJV). This is the call of the Back 2 God Movement and any person who would join us. God tells us not to be afraid of those Americans who go against His will, as He will be there for us to propel us to victory.

God has called us to do the following:

1. Root out the lies being taught in church.
2. Pull down every stronghold built against Him.
3. Destroy every evil imagination.
4. Throw down the government.
5. Build a new nation after God.
6. Plant the word of God in the hearts of all people.

Look at verses 11–13: "**Moreover the word of the Lord came to me, saying, 'Jeremiah, what do you see?' And I said, 'I see a branch of an almond tree.' Then the Lord said to me, 'You have seen well, for I am ready to perform My word.' And the word of the Lord came to me the second time, saying, 'What do you see?' And I said, 'I see a boiling pot, and it is facing away from the north'**" (NKJV). The branch of an almond tree in verse 11 suggests that God watches over Israel and promises to keep His word. The almond tree branch is actually a sign of hope. In contrast, the boiling pot in verse 13 suggests calamity is in the near future for Israel. Likewise, God offers hope to the United States of America in the form of this Back 2 God movement and through other initiatives aimed at waking up God's people. However, the calamity suggested in verse 13 could very well be this country's fate as well.

Look at verses 14–15: **"Then the Lord said to me: 'Out of the north calamity shall break forth On all the inhabitants of the land. For behold, I am calling All the families of the kingdoms of the north,' says the Lord; 'They shall come and each one set his throne At the entrance of the gates of Jerusalem, Against all its walls all around, And against all the cities of Judah'"** (NKJV). Jeremiah prophesizes that a nation out of the north, will bring great calamity to the nation of Israel. This proves to be true, as the Babylonian army comes from the North and seizes control of Israel. Is it possible that these verses suggest that God will allow a country from the north to come and cause great calamity to the United States of America?

Look at verse 16: **"I will utter My judgments Against them concerning all their wickedness, Because they have forsaken Me, Burned incense to other gods, And worshiped the works of their own hands"** (NKJV). Just as God judges the people of Israel for their wickedness in forsaking Him and worshiping other gods, is it possible that God is ready to do the same for the United States?

Look at verse 17: "**Therefore prepare yourself and arise, And speak to them all that I command you. Do not be dismayed before their faces, Lest I dismay you before them"** (NKJV). In the same way that God instructed Jeremiah to arise and speak to his nation, God is calling you and me to stand up in the Back 2 God Movement and go tell the people of this country what the Lord says! If we don't, God says He will dismay us, meaning He will bring disappointment and sadness upon us if we don't stand up for Him.

Look at verse 18**: "For behold, I have made you this day A fortified city and an iron pillar, And bronze walls against the whole land—Against**

the kings of Judah, Against its princes, Against its priests, And against the people of the land" (NKJV). God reassures Jeremiah that he will be victorious. God tells him he will be a fortified city and a bronze wall against the whole land so that he can stand up against its kings, princes, and priests. God has anointed us as His representatives of the Back 2 God Movement, and He has made us a strong tower to fight against the president, elected officials, and the pastors of this country who have rejected God.

Look at verse 19: **"'They will fight against you, But they shall not prevail against you. For I am with you,' says the Lord, 'to deliver you'"** (NKJV). Verse 19 tells us that wicked people in this nation will fight against us. Liberals will fight against us. People supporting same-sex marriage will fight against us. People supporting abortion will fight against us. God says we need to prepare for a fight, but He has already given us victory. He is with us.

Let's look at Jeremiah 2, starting with verses 1–2: "**Moreover the word of the Lord came to me, saying, 'Go and cry in the hearing of Jerusalem, saying, "Thus says the Lord: 'I remember you, The kindness of your youth, The love of your betrothal, When you went after Me in the wilderness, In a land not sown"** (NKJV). God is careful to tell Jeremiah to remind the people of Israel of the days when they faithfully followed God. He wants them to remember how God led them through the wilderness of the desert into a land flowing with milk and honey. Likewise, God is instructing us to remind Americans of their devotion to God when the country was young, how the United States was married to God, and how it followed God through the wilderness as it was birthed into a mighty nation.

Look at verse 3: **"'Israel was holiness to the Lord, The firstfruits of His increase. All that devour him will offend; Disaster will come upon them,' says the Lord"** (NKJV). God explains Israel's holiness and the status of its citizens as chosen people. He says that anyone who rises up against Israel will experience disaster and defeat. Likewise, the United States was originally holy, the apple of His eye. Anyone who rose up against us was defeated, which is how the United States became the great power it is today. God was with us.

Look at verses 4–5: "Hear the word of the Lord, O house of Jacob and all the families of the house of Israel. Thus says the Lord: 'What injustice have your fathers found in Me, That they have gone far from Me, Have followed idols, And have become idolaters?'" (NKJV). God asks Israel just what He had done to them that they would turn their backs on Him. In my sanctified imagination I can hear God saying, What did I do to you, United States, that made you go away from Me to seek after worthless things and become worthless?

Look at verse 6: **"Neither did they say, 'Where is the Lord, Who brought us up out of the land of Egypt, Who led us through the wilderness, Through a land of deserts and pits, Through a land of drought and the shadow of death, Through a land that no one crossed And where no one dwelt?'"** (NKJV). This verse tells us that no one in Israel stood up for God and asked where He had gone or remembered that He had led them to the promised land. Likewise God is saying to the United States; You did not say, 'Where is the Lord who freed us from the tyranny of England and who led us through the deserts of formation and built us into a powerful nation?

Look at verse 7: **"I brought you into a bountiful country, To eat its fruit and its goodness. But when you entered, you defiled My land And made My heritage an abomination"** (NKJV). God had brought the Israelites into Canaan, where they enjoyed the fruits and blessings of the land. Likewise, God brought us to a bountiful land, but we defile it with all types of abominations.

Look at verse 8: **"The priests did not say, 'Where is the Lord?' And those who handle the law did not know Me; The rulers also transgressed against Me; The prophets prophesied by Baal, And walked after things that do not profit"** (NKJV). God also says to us, "The church in the United States of America did not say, 'Where is God?' The pastors have moved away from Me. The government transgresses against Me. The prophets have prophesied to the love of money, power, and fame and have gone after things that do not profit."

Look at verse 9: **"'Therefore I will yet bring charges against you,' says the Lord, 'And against your children's children I will bring charges'"** (NKJV). God accuses us too, and as a result He will not only bring charges against us but also against our future generations.

Look at verse 10: **"For pass beyond the coasts of Cyprus and see, Send to Kedar and consider diligently, And see if there has been such a thing"** (NKJV). God says to search the world to see if there has ever been a nation to do a thing like this. No country has ever experienced the blessings of God in the manner that the United States has, and no country having been this blessed has ever walked away from God.

Look at verse 11: **"Has a nation changed its gods, Which are not gods? But My people have changed their Glory For what does not profit"** (NKJV). God asks whether a nation has ever changed for gods that are not gods. It is ever so clear that the United States has changed its God and the glory thereof for the riches of this world.

Look at verses 12–13: **"'Be astonished, O heavens, at this, And be horribly afraid; Be very desolate,' says the Lord. 'For My people have committed two evils: They have forsaken Me, the fountain of living waters, And hewn themselves cisterns—broken cisterns that can hold no water'"** (NKJV). Our country ought to be worried, according to God, because we have committed two evils: we have forsaken God and we have created for ourselves gods who cannot help us.

Look at verse 14: "**Is Israel a servant? Is he a homeborn slave? Why is he plundered?"** (NKJV). Is Israel a slave? Was Israel born that way? These are God's questions in this verse. Similarly God is questioning the United States of America: "Are you a slave to China and other countries? If not, then why do we need their money to survive?"

Look at verse 15: (NKJV). Is God telling us that because we've become borrowers, countries around us have seen our weakness and have begun to plot against us? Are they planning an attack on United States soil that will leave this country a wasteland, with cities burned free of inhabitants?

Look at verse 17: “ **Have you not brought this on yourself, In that you have forsaken the Lord your God When He led you in the way?”** (NKJV). We Americans have brought this situation on ourselves, simply because we walked away from the things of God.

Look at verse 18: **“And now why take the road to Egypt, To drink the waters of Sihor? Or why take the road to Assyria, To drink the waters of the River?”** (NKJV). Why even try going to China and other countries for help? It's too late. “You should have come to Me,” says the Lord.

Look at verse 19: **“‘Your own wickedness will correct you, And your backslidings will rebuke you. Know therefore and see that it is an evil and bitter thing That you have forsaken the Lord your God, And the fear of Me is not in you,’ Says the Lord God of hosts”** (NKJV). The United States is now condemned for sinning against God and for dalliances with sexual immorality, homosexuality, same-sex marriage, and government intrusion. However, the worst thing is that we don't even fear God. We think, as a nation, that we can do whatever we want and it's okay.

Look at verse 20: **“For of old I have broken your yoke and burst your bonds; And you said, ‘I will not transgress,’ When on every high hill and under every green tree You lay down, playing the harlot”** (NKJV). The United States is also charged with infidelity for worshipping money, power, and sexual gratification. Long ago this nation became a whore to these things.

Look at verse 21: **“Yet I had planted you a noble vine, a seed of highest quality. How then have you turned before Me Into the degenerate plant of an alien vine?”** (NKJV). God formed America as a godly nation, even though we didn't deserve it. How then did we turn away and make such a mess of everything?

Look at verse 22: "**'For though you wash yourself with lye, and use much soap, Yet your iniquity is marked before Me,' says the Lord God"** (NKJV). This country is so filthy with sin that no amount of soap can clean it.

Finally, look at verse 31: **"O generation, see the word of the Lord! Have I been a wilderness to Israel, Or a land of darkness? Why do My people say, 'We are lords; We will come no more to You'?"** (NKJV). God asks us the same, essentially saying, "Have I not led you, protected you, and given you power and dominion in the world? Why do you think you are now gods and do not need Me anymore?"

It's time to get back to God!

13

If My People

Just in case you're one of those people who don't believe this is your Christian responsibility, just listen to what the word of God says: **"If My people who are called by My name will humble themselves, and pray and seek My face, and turn from their wicked ways, then I will hear from heaven, and will forgive their sin and heal their land"** (2 Chronicles 7:14 NKJV). The scripture begins by saying, **"If My people who are called by My name"** … The important thing is to identify who the people are and who God is talking to. Notice that *My* is capitalized, indicating that it's God's people He's talking to. To be a Christian means that you are like Christ. Those of us who call ourselves Christians bear the name of our Lord and Savior Jesus Christ. If we bear the name of our Lord and Savior Jesus Christ, then we bear the name of God Almighty. So the "My people" in the scripture is clearly those of us who have accepted Jesus Christ as Lord and Savior.

So what is God saying to us here? Again the scripture says, **"If My people who are called by My name will *humble* themselves** …" (emphasis added). God is suggesting that we, the redeemed of the Lord, need to humble ourselves. Is it possible that we've gotten a little puffed up with pride? Is it possible that God has blessed this country so much that we've now begun to believe that we can operate on our own strength? Is it possible that because we have the largest army, navy, and marine corps, we believe we are invincible?

To continue this close analysis, the scripture says, **"If My people who are called by My name will humble themselves, and *pray* …"** (emphasis added). If God is suggesting that we need to pray, is it possible that our knees just don't hit the ground enough? Come on, you know how our prayer life goes. As long as everything in our lives is peachy and hunky-dory, our knees don't touch the ground. Oh, but let a little calamity set in. Then we're on our knees crying, begging, and pleading with God. Let us lose that great job that we had, and all of a sudden we're crying, pleading, and praying to God so hard that snot is running down our noses. Then if that doesn't work, we start lying to God. We say things like, "God, you do this for me, and I'll do that for you."

Again, the scripture says, "**If My people who are called by My name will humble themselves, and pray and *seek My face*** …" (emphasis added). If God is suggesting that we need to seek His face, is it possible that we're so busy seeking everything else in the world that we no longer seek the face of God Almighty? Is it possible that we're so busy seeking out a career that we don't seek God? Is it possible that we're so busy seeking education that we don't seek God? Ladies, is it possible that you're just so busy seeking the mall that you don't seek God? Guys, is it possible we're so busy seeking the football game or basketball game that we don't seek God?

Looking again at this quotation from scripture, it says, **""If My people who are called by My name will humble themselves, and pray and seek My face, and *turn from their wicked ways*** …" (emphasis added). This is where the rubber meets the road, because none of us would ever want to consider ourselves wicked. Let me show you how we, God's children, have been wicked. Genesis 1:26 says we were created in the image of God and that we were giving dominion over all the earth. The fact that we are God's children and have sat back and watched this country deteriorate is wicked.

Let's add one more word to our analysis: **"If My people who are called by My name will humble themselves, and pray and seek My face, and turn from their wicked ways, *then* …"** (emphasis added). If you truly understand this scripture, you are jumping up and down and shouting for joy because of the word *then*. *Then* is the transition word. God is clearly saying to us that if we will do the things that come before *then,* He will do everything that comes after *then.* So if we will humble ourselves, pray, seek God's face, and turn from our wicked ways, then God says He will hear from heaven. You need to understand that Jesus is talking now, because Jesus sits at the right hand of the Father, making intercessions for you and me. I can hear Jesus in my sanctified imagination saying to God the Father, "Please, Father, give the United States of America one more chance. Father, I believe if you give them one more chance they will not turn their backs on You again."

So God says that if we will humble ourselves, pray, seek His face, and turn from our wicked ways, not only will He hear from heaven, but he will forgive our sins. That's really good news for me, because unlike some of my other Christian brothers and sisters, I did not come out of my mother's womb saved! I need God to forgive me for the ways I have not stood up for Him.

Lastly, the scripture says that if we do all the aforementioned things, not only will He hear from heaven and forgive our sins, but God also promises to heal our land. For those of you who think the *land* this scripture refers to is dirt, let me help you out.

"The land" refers to our schools. God says if we will humble ourselves and pray, seek His face, and turn from our wicked ways, He is ready to go into our school system and make a crooked place straight.

"The land" refers to our communities. God says if we will humble ourselves, pray, seek His face, and turn from our wicked ways, He's ready to go into our communities that are infested with sin and turn them right side up with the gospel.

"The land" refers to our government. God says if we will humble ourselves, pray, seek His face, and turn from our wicked ways, He is ready to go into our government. The government is not too big for Him. Even now God is willing and able to take that crooked system infested with sin and lies and turn it into a godly system that honors Him.

God is willing, able, and ready to receive the United States of America back. It's up to you and me as children of the most high God to remind our brothers and sisters that the time is here and the time is now for us to stand together to profess and confess that Jesus Christ is Lord. The time is here and the time is now for us to stand up to this corrupt government and tell corrupt politicians that they don't represent us. The time is here and the time is now for us to stand up to the Supreme Court and tell them that we will not obey laws that they send down if those laws go against God's laws.

Time and time again God has allowed His people to experience suffering and pain, only to provide an opportunity for us to come to our senses and return to Him. I pray that this book empowers you to do just that: stand up for God in your individual lives and in this nation.

After all, it's up to you and me to lead this nation back to God as part of the Back 2 God Movement!

Printed in the United States
By Bookmasters